Helion & Company Limited
Unit 8 Amherst Business Centre
Budbrooke Road
Warwick
CV34 5WE
England
Tel. 01926 499 619
Email: info@helion.co.uk
Website: www.helion.co.uk
Twitter: @helionbooks
Visit our blog http://blog.helion.co.uk/

CONTENTS

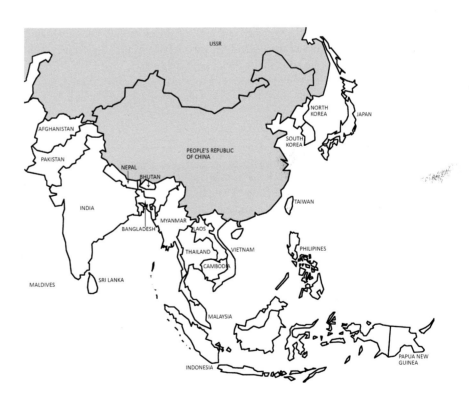

Note: In order to simplify the use of this book, all names, locations and geographic designations are as provided in *The Times World Atlas*, or other traditionally accepted major sources of reference, as of the time of described events.

ABBREVIATIONS

AK	Kalashnikov assault rifle (*avtomat Kalashnikova*)
AKM	modernised Kalashnikov assault rifle (*avtomat Kalashnikova modernizirovannyi*)
APC	armoured personnel carrier (*BTR* or *Bronetransporter*)
CC	Central Committee
CPC	Communist Party of China
CPSU	Communist Party of the Soviet Union
FSB	Federal Security Service (*Federalnaya sluzhba bezopasnosti*)
GDR	German Democratic Republic
KGB	Committee of State Security (*Komitet gosudarstvennoy besopasnosti*)
MFA	Ministry of Foreign Affairs
MRD	motorised rifle division
NP	observation post (*nablyudatelnyi punkt*)
PLA	People's Liberation Army (China)
POW	prisoner of war
PRC	People's Republic of China
RF	Russian Federation
RPD	Degtyarev light machine gun (*ruchnoy pulemet Degtyareva*)
RPG	light antitank grenade launcher (*ruchnoy protivotankovyi grenatomet*)
RPK	Kalashnikov light machine gun (*ruchnoy pulemet Kalashnikova*)
RSFSR	Russian Soviet Federative Socialist Republic
RViA	rocket troops and artillery (*raketnye voyska i artilleriya*)
SKS	Simonov self-loading carbine (*samozaryadnyi karabin Simonova*)
US(A)	United States (of America)
USSR	Union of Soviet Socialist Republics (colloquially 'Soviet Union')

ACKNOWLEDGEMENTS

We would like to express our sincere thanks to the veterans who directly took part in the events of 1969: A.D. Konstantinov, Yu.V. Babansky, N.I. Popov, V.D. Pavlyuk, N.A. Zadorozhny, G.M. Zhestkov, A.V. Shamov, V.M. Tirskikh, A.I. Nikitin, N.A. Rozhkov, V.V. Puchkov, Ye.B. Govor, A.A. Murzin, and A.I. Tsogla. These men agreed to meet and talk personally or entered into fruitful correspondence with the authors.

We thank the directors of the Foundation for the Support of Veterans of the Border Guards, 'Vernost', and also the directors of the Central Border Museum of the Federal Security Service of the Russian Federation for permission to use their photo archives.

We would like to express our appreciation to A.A. Sabadash, Ye.D. Leonova, O.N. Bykova, V.N. Volik, S.P. Vashenyak, A.L. Volkov, A.D. Leonkin, A.N. Musalov, V.I. Gladkov, G.V. Kravchenko, D.V. Kiselev, Reiko Nishioka (Japan), and Elizabeth McGuire (USA) for the materials they provided.

Several citizens of the People's Republic of China rendered generous assistance in the work on this book, selflessly providing many Chinese materials. Complying with their request, we will not identify them by name; nevertheless, we wish to express our sincere gratitude to them.

The Authors

EDITORIAL NOTE

As with the first volume of this work the translation, undertaken by Dr Orenstein, is a faithful reproduction in English of the original Russian text. In order to preserve the authenticity of that text the editors have taken a very light hand to the manuscript in order to avoid any unwarranted changes of inflection or meaning.

1
15 MARCH 1969

Reinforced Soviet border guard details continuously arrived on Damansky Island after the 2 March events.[1] As a rule, officers headed these details. Border guards on armoured personnel carriers (APCs) were continuously on the spit located opposite the southern end of Damansky. Sappers from a separate sapper battalion mined the island in case of an attack by Chinese infantry.

An operations group, made up of officers from the Pacific Ocean Border District headquarters, was created for the purpose of directing the combat operations. Located at the Nizhne-Mikhaylovka Outpost, the group was headed by Colonel G.P. Sechkin, the deputy chief of the border district's troops.

KGB Chairman Yu.V. Andropov, who was responsible for the border troops, signed the order about reinforcing the Iman Border Detachment, in accordance with which the detachment obtained Mi-4 helicopters (one flight) and manoeuvre groups from the Kamen-Rybolov and Grodekov Border Detachments.

In assessing the situation on the border, the Soviet command concluded that it was necessary to reinforce the border troops with regular Soviet Army units. There were such units in the Far Eastern Military District's 45th Army Corps.

The formation of the corps had begun two years before the events on Damansky, when, in spring 1967, a large group of officers and generals from Crimea arrived in the Far East. General V.I. Bulgakov commanded the corps; in 1968 he was replaced by General S.A. Rzhechitsky, who before this had served in the Novorossiysk Motorised Rifle Division (MRD). Corps headquarters was located in Lesozavodsk.

135th MRD, which had come to Primorye from Artemovsk (Ukraine, Donetsk Oblast), was part of 45th Army Corps. At this time, 199th Verkhne-Udinsky Regiment, which was part of the division, was already located in the village of Filino.

In addition to 135th MRD, the corps had at its disposal the Imam Fortified Region and construction units.[2] The corps' area of responsibility stretched from Guberovo (right flank) to Lake Khanka (left flank).

After the first battle on 2 March, 135th MRD (commanded by General Major V.K. Nesov) – infantry, tanks, artillery, and 'Grad' multiple launch rocket systems – was deployed in the rear several kilometres from Damansky. Another army operations group, headed by Colonel N.A. Yegerev, was organised to coordinate operations with the border guards.

Colonel D.V. Leonov, chief of the Iman Border Detachment, received two motorised rifle companies (from 135th MRD's 199th Motorised Rifle Regiment), two tank platoons, and two mortar platoons. He was assigned the following task: in case of a Chinese attack, to hold Damansky using all available forces. If the conflict escalated into a battle, 135th MRD units were to be committed, in which case overall command was to be transferred to General Nesov. Nesov had been ordered to prepare beforehand a massive artillery strike against the enemy if the border guards were forced to leave the island and the Chinese occupied it. It was particularly emphasised that fire was to be conducted only on Damansky; shells were not to be allowed to burst on Chinese territory. Any combat operations without an order from the commander of the Far East Military District were strictly prohibited.

The Chinese also were not dozing: they assembled as much as a PLA regiment in the Damansky area. The precise make-up of the Chinese troops is still not known; however, information on the Chinese Internet makes it possible to assume, that subunits from 201st and 202nd Regiments of the PLA took part in the battle that ensued. Considerable artillery support forces were assembled here.

The Soviet border guards attentively followed what was happening on Chinese territory. It was established that mass rallies, with the participation of Chinese servicemen, had taken place in populated border areas, at which 'Repel the Soviet revisionists' could be heard. The arrivals of Chinese reconnaissance groups at the border were noted, from which it followed that a new battle for Damansky was brewing.

The authors of some Russian publications about the fighting on Damansky are not too respectful – one might even say they were contemptuous – when they spoke about the Chinese soldiers:

Lieutenant Colonel Ye.I. Yanshin. (from V.N. Volik)

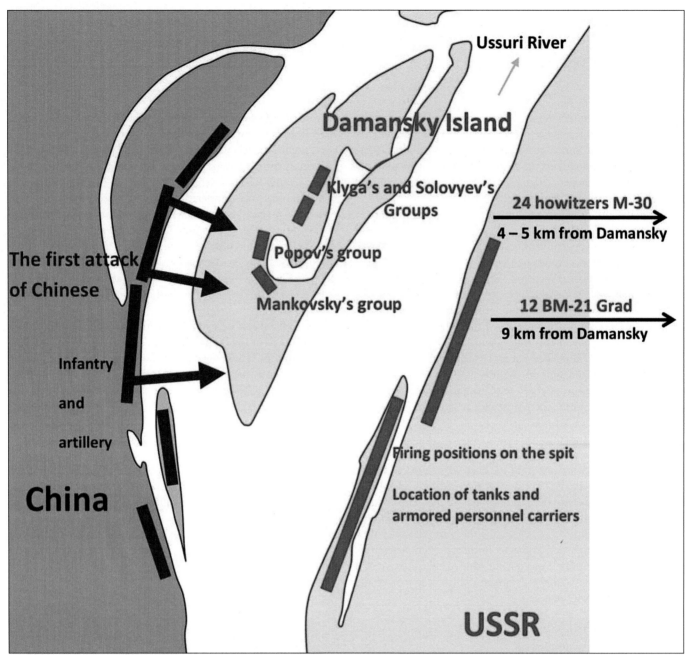

Sketch Map 3. The beginning of the battle on 15 March 1969. (Sketch maps 1 and 2 appear in Volume 1. Map drawn by authors)

they said that these soldiers served in an agricultural division and, therefore, had not mastered military skills.

In fact, the system of equipping the armed forces in China was quite unique. An important component of this system was the agriculture divisions, which comprised local inhabitants. Under usual conditions these men worked in the fields or were involved in other completely peaceful activities; if necessary, however, they took up arms. These weapons – just as with ammunition, uniforms, transport, food and water – were stored in places where Chinese citizens permanently resided, that is, there were always at hand. Upon receiving a certain signal or command, the peaceful peasants in the blink of an eye turned into numerous, well-armed military subunits. It should be added that combat exercises were regularly held and strict discipline maintained in the agricultural divisions; therefore, a contemptuous attitude toward these formations was in no way justified. What must really be acknowledged is the Soviets' superiority in the quality of their individual types of combat equipment; however, this fact is explained by the general underdevelopment of the PLA when compared with the Soviet

Army. Furthermore, it should not be forgotten that for the entire time the Chinese had overwhelming numerical superiority. The main thing is that in the subsequent 15 March battle only regular PLA troops took part, while soldiers in the agricultural divisions played a secondary role – they delivered ammunition, carried off the wounded, etc.

With the considerable concentration of opposing forces in the Damansky area, only a political decision at the highest level could have prevented new bloodshed. Judging by everything, the Chinese leadership was simply not ready for a diplomatic settlement, and thus brought this conflict to a logical conclusion.

On 14 March at around 15:00, the Iman Border Detachment received an order: remove the details from the island. The logic and purpose of this order are still not clear, just as the person who gave the order is still not known (nevertheless, Soviet veterans are of the opinion that General V.F. Lobanov, chief of the Pacific Ocean Border District, issued the order. And this is why: no one even suggests this in a purely hypothetical sense).

Chinese artillery fires on Damansky, 15 March 1969. (Military Museum of Hanoi, via Albert Grandolini)

The border troops withdrew from Damansky, and the Chinese riverbank immediately became animated. Some groups of 10–15 soldiers each began to run in the direction of the river; others occupied trenches opposite the island and set up machine guns and grenade launchers; still others redeployed along the border. Several Chinese servicemen, dressed in camouflage, crawled over to Damansky and then returned to the Chinese riverbank.

The air reconnaissance that the Soviets conducted detected a large number of campfires on the Chinese side, around 10 kilometres from Damansky. It was assumed that this was a concentration of infantry about the size of a battalion. At the same time, technical equipment for listening to any sounds on the island showed that there were no Chinese on Damansky.

At around 03:30 a.m. (15 March), a new order arrived from General Lobanov: occupy the island. Lieutenant Colonel Ye.I. Yanshin, at that time the commander of a motorised manoeuvre group of the Iman Border Detachment, was assigned this task.

At 05:30 a.m. Yanshin's detachment arrived at the island in four APCs. There were 45 border guards in this detachment. Around 50 soldiers and officers in three APCs were deployed on the Russian riverbank to support Yanshin's group; Colonel Leonov was also located here. At the same time, two motorised rifle companies and a mortar battery were located at Mount Kafyla and Mount Krestovaya. The border guards at Nizhne-Mikhaylovka Outpost itself were armed with antitank weapons, in case of an attack by Chinese tanks. There were also around 100 reserves located here.

Yanshin's soldiers were deployed in four groups, about 100 metres apart from one another. They had dug shallow trenches (see Sketch Map 3). Officers L. Mankovsky, N. Popov, V. Solovyev, and A. Klyga commanded the groups. The APCs were continuously moving around the island, changing their positions.

At around 08:00 on 15 March, a loudspeaker began to operate. A ringing female voice called upon the Soviet border guards in Russian to leave 'Chinese territory', to 'reject revisionism', etc. Petr Ivanovich Kosinov – at that time a major and deputy chief of staff of the Grodekov Border Detachment – recalled the following:

As soon as the propaganda apparatus on the Chinese riverbank began broadcasting, Leonov said to Konstantinov, "Aleksandr Dmitriyevich, well, let's get your barrel organ out." He had in mind our loudspeaker station with a text that had been written down in Chinese.

However, when our men tried to turn on this "barrel organ," the engine began to sneeze, as Leonov put it. Now it started up, now it stalled. In a fit of anger, he muttered, "Yes, our counterpropaganda is powerful."

The incident was saved. Among us was a comrade from Moscow. He knew Chinese. This comrade grabbed the megaphone and began to speak Chinese.[3]

The broadcast was made using rather simple words: think about it before it's too late; before you are the sons of those who liberated China from the Japanese invaders. They gave a friendly warning about responsibility in case hostile actions continued.

At around 10:00, an announcer began to speak Chinese, and, judging from the intensity and volume, he was addressing the PLA soldiers with an inspiring speech.

Sometime later there was silence on both sides, but around 10:00 Chinese artillery and mortars began to shell the island. A Chinese infantry company (100–150 men) began to attack. In groups of 10–12 men the Chinese ran across the channel and joined the battle (as Chinese observers recorded, the PLA soldiers rushed to Damansky at 10:02).

N. I. Popov recalled the following:

At around 10 o'clock in the morning the Chinese opened heavy artillery and mortar fire. The first Chinese soldiers appeared on the southern part of the island. There was more than a company of them.

When the Chinese came closer to us, my group was the first to join the battle. Four of our armoured personnel carriers conducted machine gun fire while moving.

Suddenly I saw: Chinese soldiers were running directly at us. The machine gunner was firing long bursts. And we could be seen in full view from the Chinese riverbank. The shooting was crazy. I was wearing a new fur coat, and all the flaps were in tatters. But I didn't even have [a] scratch.

Yanshin quickly understood what was going on; he turned his armoured personnel carrier and covered us.[4]

Chinese positions on Damansky, 15 March 1969. (Chinese Internet)

Colonel Sechkin reported the situation to the border district and Far East Military District headquarters, saying the observers from 135th MRD's artillery regiment had detected the location of Chinese mortar batteries and artillery, which were ready to quickly open fire. The one thing needed was permission, but there was none.

The fierce fighting lasted around one hour. Despite strong shelling, Soviet border guard casualties were minimal: a total of five wounded, none killed. Communications were lost between Yanshin and the riverbank: it was explained later that antennas on the APCs were cut by their own machine-gun fire from the rotating turrets.

By 11:00 the defenders' ammunition had begun to run out, and three APCs had been damaged. Under these conditions, Yanshin decided to leave the island for a while in order to carry off the wounded, replace the APCs, and replenish ammunition. The Chinese, seeing the withdrawal of the border guards from Damansky, quickly occupied positions along the bank in the southern and western parts of the island.

Colonel Leonov assigned Yanshin and Kosinov the task of going to the island again, holding their positions, preventing the enemy from spreading out further, and, if feasible, driving the Chinese from Damansky (in the general opinion of the veterans of the battle, the latter was already impossible, inasmuch as the Chinese had established a strong defence, equipped with antitank resources, along the riverbank).

P. I. Kosinov recalled the following:

Around half past eleven we arrived at the bank along the channel. We encountered heavy fire: mine explosions, shooting from grenade launchers, machine-gun bursts. We remembered our main task: don't allow the enemy to spread out. But there was one more important task: don't let them set our APCs on fire.

My APC was on the far right. On the left was Petrov's vehicle. He got carried away, and in the heat of the attack moved closer than one hundred metres. His APC ignited when a shell hit it. I immediately ordered my men to move forward, because I saw that soldiers were jumping out of Petrov's APC. On the left flank they also began to move toward it and cover it with fire. …

Having moved up about 35 metres, I saw several dead men; someone was crawling in the snow, others were jumping from the side and returning fire. Then an explosion roared from Petrov's APC. Most likely a shell had hit the gas tank. Realising that no one was left there, I gave the order to stop and covered those who were crawling away from the APC with fire. And now a shell hit the right side of our APC. …

After the 15 March 1969 battle. Ilya Kobets is seen on the left. (Military Museum of Hanoi, via Albert Grandolini)

A bright orange burst in my eyes, an explosion of awesome force, a jolt in my legs.[5]

Once again, communications between Leonov and Yanshin were lost; however, the command post heard the conversations between the APCs that were taking part in the battle: two vehicles had burned and there were dead. The chief of the border detachment realised

Tanks from Leonov's group on the Ussuri ice. (Chinese Internet)

command tank blew up on a mine. Leonov and some of the crew were wounded. Having left the tank, they made their way to their riverbank. Here, a Chinese bullet struck Leonov. Three of the other vehicles were damaged and left on the Ussuri ice for the Nizhne-Mikhaylovka Outpost.

The fighting on the island took on a sporadic character: disparate groups of border guards continued to attack and repel the Chinese, who were significantly superior numerically to the defenders. Several tanks that were also involved in the battle substantially helped the border guards. Despite all the reinforcements, however, the numerical superiority of the Chinese was very sizeable: approximately 10:1. Nevertheless, subunits from 135th Division continued to play the ludicrous role of mere observers, and did not intervene in the events.

that his available forces would not be able to drive the Chinese off the island. In addition, the question arose about the overwhelming Chinese forces seizing Damansky. Leonov reported to his superior about the enemy's numerically greater forces and the necessity of using artillery, but he received no support. Obviously the command did not dare take such measures as the situation required.

At one time during the battle observers noticed that the Chinese had begun to group on their riverbank opposite the southern tip of the island: 400–500 soldiers clearly intended to strike the Soviet border guards' flank.

In order to thwart the enemy's plan, I. Kobets' grenade launcher team opened SPG-9 fire from its own riverbank. Machine gunners were also firing from here. Under the complex conditions, however, this was inadequate. Colonel Leonov then decided to carry out a raid on four tanks (Leonov had been promised a tank company on 13 March, but nine vehicles from 135th MRD's 152nd Separate Tank Battalion had arrived only in the midst of the battle).

There was possibly another reason, which Aleksandr Dmitriyevich Konstantinov, former chief of the political department of the Iman Border Detachment, recalled:

He spoke on the telephone with someone at the command post in Nizhne-Mikhaylovka. As I understood from the conversation, he was being blamed for the fact that the fighting had already been going on for two hours, but he had not been able to take a captive. It seemed to me (we did not have a chance to properly talk about it) that is why he set off for the island in a tank. It was a tragic mistake: Demokrat Vladimirovich was in the first tank. A commander never rides in the head tank. Especially on the left side, facing the Chinese riverbank.[6]

Leonov was in the head vehicle and four T-62s moved in the direction of the southern tip of Damansky.[7] At the same time, border guards and motorised riflemen attacked the island, and the fighting erupted with new intensity.

It was approximately in this place, where the distance between the Chinese riverbank and the island was minimal, that the

One of the eyewitnesses to the events recalled how Lieutenant Colonel Konstantinov called the army command post after Leonov's death. Ignoring the rank and position of those to whom he was talking, Konstantinov spoke from the heart to the inactive command. While the latter themselves had been eager for battle, being bound by discipline, they were unable to do anything, and no order had been given.

Former nurse N.A. Tsymbal recalled the following:

The wounded began to arrive during the second half of the day, and we continued to receive them until the middle of the night. Many were burned, concussed, and had bullet wounds. A helicopter brought the soldiers, landing directly in front of the hospital. We needed a lot of blood. We performed immediate triage so as to help those who still could be helped. Unfortunately, this was not always successful.[8]

After 14:00, around 200 Chinese ran across to Damansky. They then continued to come in large groups, and the firing almost stopped. The Soviets perceived this as preparation to destroy Yanshin's group and seize the entire island. A mortar battery from 135th MRD opened fire along the channel between Damansky and the Chinese riverbank, but all this was not enough to repel the expected enemy attack.

Thus, the real threat of losing Damansky arose. It became obvious that a command decision had to be made quickly.

However, none of those invested with power wanted to take the responsibility on himself – neither the division command, nor the district command, nor the generals from the Ministry of Defence and General Staff. Everyone understood that in case of complications one could lose not only one's position and rank, but also something more serious. As for the top officials of the state, General Secretary of the CC CPSU L.I. Brezhnev was on his way to Budapest as head

The wounded are taken away on a helicopter during the 15 March 1969 battle. (Military Museum of Hanoi, via Albert Grandolini)

of delegation to participate in the work of the Warsaw Pact's Political Advisory Committee.[9]

Aleksandr Leonidovich Knyazev (in March 1969 a sergeant and deputy commander of a radio platoon of a control and artillery reconnaissance battery of 135th MRD) recalled the following:

The division commander, chief of division artillery, senior division officers, and subunit commanders who had taken up their line of departure along the border gathered at the command post. They were also observing what was happening and quietly exchanged opinions. Division Commander General Major Nesov ordered that he be put through to the commander of the Far East Military District. After reporting about the situation on the island, he asked for permission to conduct fire support by artillery for the subunits that were already fighting against the enemy. In reply he received an order not to open fire and not to send anyone but border guards to the island. They were waiting for an order from Moscow.[10]

There are two basic versions about who finally made the decision.

The first version: the decision was made by Brezhnev, to whom the escort reported about the situation – Damansky casualties, losses, etc. Allegedly struck by this news, the General Secretary called the generals and ordered them in no uncertain terms to use all resources on hand to liberate the island.

The second version: the decision to deliver a strike against the Chinese riverbank was made by then Commander of the Far East Military District, General O.A. Losik.

With the first version it is more or less clear: if Brezhnev did, in fact, give the order, then the military simply 'saluted' and carried out the will of the leadership. In this case the instructions to engage artillery should have come to the scene of the events from the General Staff.

As for the second version, Losik probably phoned Moscow and asked for precise instructions, but did not receive them (what is more, it was early morning abroad and in Moscow, and not all the General Staff leaders were at work). The situation in the Damansky area, however, continued to worsen, and the commander of the Far Eastern Military District was literally forced to make a decision on his own. Thus, accusations of General Losik's procrastination and

his decisiveness at this most crucial moment fit into this version of the events.

At one time there was talk that General I.G. Pavlovsky, commander-in-chief of the Ground Forces and deputy minister of defence, had given the order to Losik about striking the Chinese riverbank. Pavlovsky allegedly had arrived several days later at the scene, where he heard reports by the commanders who had taken part in the battle.

It can now be said with complete assurance that Pavlovsky issued no instructions to the commander of the Red Banner Far East Military District. As for his coming to the scene after the events, this is true. He was, indeed, in the area of the island and talked with officers who had taken part in the battle.

There is yet another version of the above-mentioned order, one that is quite probable. The fact is that one of the authors of this book spoke with General P.M. Plotnikov in Moscow in summer 2004. In 1969 Plotnikov held the position of first deputy commander of the Red Banner Far East Military District. On 15 March 1969 he was at the scene of the events and, moreover, was the senior ranking officer there. In any case, he declared that it was he who gave the order for a massive strike against the Chinese. He had not coordinated this critical decision with anyone, having taken this step because the Chinese were continuously shelling Damansky.

Plotnikov said that a few minutes after the artillery strike against the Chinese, Minister of Defence Grechko called him. Assuming that he was now going to be removed from his position, Plotnikov reported about what had happened. However, Grechko only briefly jumped in: 'Go easy on your ammunition there', and with this the conversation ended.

At first glance, Grechko's words seem strange, even ridiculous; with more thoughtful analysis, however, they are completely logical. After all, Grechko did not know what consequences General Plotnikov's decision would have for him personally; therefore, he expressed himself in a way so that, regardless of any development of events, he was in a win-win situation.

For example, if the use of mass artillery fire resulted in the cessation of the battle, then Grechko would report to Brezhnev that at the most critical moment of the battle he called the scene, accepted a report, gave advice to effectively use costly ammunition, etc. If Plotnikov's decision led to a widening of the conflict, then Grechko would report differently: having found out about General Plotnikov's incorrect actions, he [Grechko] immediately called the scene, accepted a report, severely reprimanded the general for an unjustified expenditure of costly ammunition, etc. Thus, either way, Grechko was able to present his actions in the most favourable light and obtain Brezhnev's approval.

It is entirely possible that the order for the artillery strike against Chinese territory was issued – with a small difference in time – by both Plotnikov and Losik. Lately, it has been possible to examine the records of orders and telephone conversations which took place

MT-LB tractors tow D-1 howitzers to Damansky. (Military Museum of Hanoi, via Albert Grandolini)

during the battle on 15 March 1969. As a result, the order to open artillery fire along the Chinese riverbank came from the General Staff, meaning that General Losik was just following the order from Moscow. However, regardless of who, in fact, was the author of this order, the approval obtained from above made it possible for the Soviet commanders to act more meaningfully and purposefully.

At that time, 135th MRD's organic artillery consisted of the following:

1. 378th Artillery Regiment minus 3rd, 6th, and 9th Batteries (military unit No. 40888; regiment commander – Lieutenant Colonel V.P. Borisenko). On the day of the battle the regiment had 24 M-30 122mm howitzers and 12 D-1 152mm howitzers;

2. 13th Separate Rocket Artillery Battalion minus 3rd Battery (battalion commander – Major M.T. Vashchenko). The battalion had 12 BM-21 'Grad' rocket launchers in the Damansky area;

3. a separate antitank battalion with T-12 100mm cannons (battalion commander – Senior Lieutenant V. Abramov). Two of the three batteries (twelve cannons) were deployed.

By 15:00–15:30, 378th Artillery Regiment's first and second artillery battalions, each armed with 12 M-30 122mm howitzers, were at their fire positions, 4–5 kilometres east of Damansky Island. At this time the third regimental battalion was still only moving to the fire position area, and there was a reason for that. The fact is that the fire position area for the third artillery battalion was planned for four kilometres northeast of Damansky Island. The battalion's fire subunits, which had descended from the steep slope of the northeast spur of Mount Krasnaya, had moved to the indicated area. Having arrived at the fire position area, the battalion discovered that the place could be easily seen from the Chinese riverbank, and reported this to the higher command. The artillery regiment command identified a new fire position area for the third battalion. The battalion's artillery batteries had to turn back and move in the opposite direction. However, the automobiles and howitzer tractors were unable to overcome the steep icy incline, and rolled down. This continued for 30–40 minutes, until a group of soldiers on one of the tractors went around the pass on virgin soil, thereby laying a path

for the remaining vehicles. This all took time; therefore, it was later that 3rd Battalion finally arrived at the scene, with 378th Artillery Regiment's 1st and 2nd Battalions already firing against the enemy. Eyewitnesses recall that the gun teams were so hot from the fighting that some soldiers stripped to their waist, to their underwear, and this when the temperature was around -10°C.

By 15 March, 13th Separate Rocket Artillery Battalion was already deployed in combat formation. The battalion command and observation post was deployed on the southwestern slopes of Mount Kafyla, and the fire positions of the rocket batteries were nine kilometres east of Damansky. Two days before the battle the battalion had been engaged in exercises; therefore, the march to the area of the island had been very strenuous. Mikhail Tikhonovich Vashchenko recalled the following:

In the evening of the thirteenth we returned to the barracks. It was already the end of the day. … The guys were ready to go and rest and put the equipment in its place. I was called to the corps commander. There it so happened that the corps itself was located next to us in Lesozavodsk, immediately in the town of Medvednitsky, while the division commander was closer to the north, about 70 kilometres from there. Well, Corps Commander General Lieutenant Rzhechitsky assigned the task: move north, take everything for readiness, as he said, "for long life and training under field conditions." This was understood. All the time we always had everything with us. I had to return the soldiers to the parks. I soon gathered the officers and junior commanders and told them what was what. … We took the necessary stock of topographic maps, food, and dry rations for four days. And we set out. It was just night, that is, the thirteenth and fourteenth [of March]. Night. Although there were tired soldiers among us. Especially the drivers. The officers too. But we handled it.[11]

At 17:00, two artillery battalions, the separate rocket battalion, and a 120mm mortar battery from 199th Motorised Rifle Regiment opened fire against areas of concentration of Chinese troops and their fire positions. Despite the widely disseminated myth that Soviet artillery wiped Damansky from the face of the Earth, fire was conducted predominantly against the Chinese riverbank, inasmuch as scattered groups of border guards remained on Damansky.

The 'Grad' launchers. (Military Museum of Hanoi, via Albert Grandolini)

The vehicles entered the channel, after which the Soviet soldiers hurried and deployed in the direction of the rampart along the western riverbank (see Sketch Map 4). This flank manoeuvre was made because, if the Chinese had made a frontal attack, they would have been able to disable the APCs with soldiers inside, which would have resulted in casualties.

Although they lost fire support from their riverbank, the Chinese, nevertheless, continued to resist fiercely. Finally, under pressure from the Soviet soldiers, the invaders were forced to abandon the island. At around 18:30, Damansky was completely liberated, but sometime later some Chinese fire positions revived. It is possible that for the complete destruction of the enemy the Soviet soldiers would have had to conduct one more fire raid; the appropriate command did not, however, arrive.

The Chinese tried again to seize Damansky, but their attacks failed completely. After this the Soviet soldiers withdrew to their riverbank, while the Chinese made no more attempts to capture the island: obviously, they understood that the Soviet command was very serious, and that further continuation would be deadly for the Chinese.

The raid was exceptionally precise: shells destroyed the Chinese reserves, mortars, shell stockpiles, etc. Information from radio interception attested to the hundreds of dead enemy soldiers and commanders. Eyewitnesses recalled how sharply the picture had changed on that bank of the Ussuri: bustling and firing before the salvo from the rocket battalion and complete absence of any movement after.

The artillery fired for 10 minutes, and at 17:10 motorised riflemen attacked. One hundred and twenty soldiers from 199th Motorised Rifle Regiment's 2nd Motorised Rifle Battalion on 12 APCs (commander – Lieutenant Colonel Aleksandr Ivanovich Smirnov) and 80 border guards on 6 APCs (commander – Chief of the Political Department of the Iman Border Detachment Lieutenant Colonel Aleksandr Dmitriyevich Konstantinov) took part in the attack. Five tanks supported the attack.

Even now the reason for the pause between the end of the artillery raid and the beginning of the attack is unknown. The Chinese took advantage of this and sent reinforcements to the island.

On the same day, the Soviet government sent the following note of protest to the PRC government, in which the 15 March 1969 events were assessed:

Declaration of the Soviet Government to the Government of the People's Republic of China

The government of the Union of Soviet Socialist Republics declares the following to the government of the People's Republic of China

On 14 March 1969 at 11.15, Moscow time, a group of armed Chinese soldiers undertook a new attempt to invade Soviet territory – Damansky Island on the Ussuri River. The next day, 15 March, a large armed detachment of Chinese soldiers, supported from the riverbank by artillery and mortar fire, attacked Soviet border guards, who were patrolling the island, as a result of which there were dead and wounded. Measures were taken to force the

Damansky under fire, 15 March 1969. (Chinese Internet)

in the Damansky Island area, a provocation that was deliberately calculated to create an atmosphere of estrangement between the people of the PRC and the USSR, the Soviet Government warns that all responsibility for possible serious consequences of similar reckless actions on the part of the Chinese authorities lies squarely on the Chinese.

Moscow, 15 March 1969[12]

In the 15 March battle, 17 border guards died – 3 from the Iman Border Detachment (indicated by an asterisk in the list below) and 14 from Kamen-Rybolov Border Detachment (military unit 2097, village of Komissarovo). The following is a list of their names: Private Tofik Rza-Ogly Abbasov, Private Yuri Yuryevich Akhmetshin, Private Vladimir Tarasovich Bildushkinov*, Junior Sergeant Vladimir Konstantinovich Gayunov, Private Sergey Viktorovich Gladyshev, Sergeant Boris Aleksandrovich Golovin, Senior Sergeant Anvar Akkhiyamovich Zaynutdinov, Private Anatoly Mikhaylovich Kovalev, Colonel Demokrat Vladimirovich Leonov*, Junior Sergeant Vladimir Yuryevich Malykhin, Senior Lieutenant Lev Konstantinovich Mankovsky*, Private Viktor Petrovich Solyanik, Private Dmitry Vladimirovich Tkachenko, Private Aleksey Ivanovich Chechenin, Private Vitaly Gilionovich Shamsutdinov, Private Stanislav Fedorovich Yurin, Private Anatoly Iosifovich Yakovlev.

Seven servicemen from 135th MRD died in this same battle: Private Aleksandr Vasilyevich Bedarev, Private Aleksandr Khristianovich Gelvikh, Private Sergey Timofeyevich Koltakov, Private Aleksey Alekseyevich Kuzmin, Junior Sergeant Vladimir Viktorovich Orekhov, Private Vladimir Vasilyevich Potapov, Private Vladimir Timofeyevich Shtoyko.

Six burned APCs and one tank (No. 545) comprised the equipment losses.

In the above list, special mention should be given to Junior Sergeant Vladimir Orekhov, inasmuch as he was awarded (posthumously) the Hero of the Soviet Union medal. A street was named after him in Komsomolsk-na-Amure, and an individual display is dedicated to him in Russia's Central Museum of the Armed Forces. For a long time, Orekhov's name was not mentioned in the USSR, because Soviet authorities did not want to admit that Soviet Army units were taking part in the border conflict. So why was such a high honour conferred on Orekhov?

A.I. Nikitin, former deputy chief of 45th Army Corps' political department, had kept a curious document. It was a handwritten draft of an order from Colonel D.A. Krupeynikov, commander of 199th Regiment, dated 16 March 1969. The draft was written with a black ballpoint pen on a standard double sheet from a school notebook. Several names of those who died were added with a blue pencil, and the name 'Orekhov' was underlined. Here is the text of this order:[13]

Order of the motorised rifle regiment 16 March 1969 No. Nizhne-Mikhaylovka post

provocateurs off the island. This new, naked, armed aggression by Chinese authorities is fraught with serious consequences.

At the same time, official Chinese organs are intensifying anti-Soviet hysteria around unjustified and aggressive territorial claims, attempting to create the foundation for new exacerbation of tension in Sino-Soviet inter-governmental relations. Crudely perverting the facts, they are attempting to evade the responsibility for ventures on the Sino-Soviet border that were planned and organized beforehand.

The facts say that the government of the People's Republic of China did not make the necessary conclusions from the Soviet government's warning regarding the 2 March 1969 armed provocation, organised by the Chinese authorities, on Damansky Island and continues to provoke new incidents.

During a 12 March 1969 meeting between representatives of the Soviet and Chinese border guards, officers from the Hutou Chinese Border Post, citing instructions from Mao Zedong, threatened the employment of armed force in regard to the Soviet border guards patrolling Damansky Island.

The Soviet government decisively rejects the Chinese authorities' unfounded claims.

Damansky Island is an integral part of Soviet territory. The false statements advanced on this matter by the Chinese authorities are nothing more than an attempt to mislead public opinion in China and other countries.

The Soviet government considers it necessary to emphasize in no uncertain terms that the borders of the Soviet Union are sacred and inviolable. The Soviet government declares once again that it is decisively against military confrontation on the Sino-Soviet border. All of Peking's propaganda statements on the hostility of the Soviet Union and the CPSU toward the People's Republic of China are absolutely groundless. The Soviet Union seeks no confrontations; on the contrary, it is taking all measures to avoid them.

In addition, the Soviet government declares that if the legal rights of the USSR are trampled, if future attempts are undertaken to violate the inviolability of Soviet territory, then the Union of Soviet Socialist Republics and all its people will resolutely defend it and crushingly repel such violations.

In announcing this strict protest to the government of the People's Republic of China because of this new provocation

Substance: On praising the personnel of 2nd MRB for bravery and heroism exhibited in the defence of the borders of our Motherland.

On 15 March 1969 at 17:00, 2nd MRB, cooperating with a border detachment, took part in the liberation of Damansky Isl. from the Chinese invaders.

In carrying out the Motherland's order to defend the Far Eastern borders, officers, sergeants, and enlisted exhibited exceptional bravery and heroism in the battles to liberate Damansky Isl. and accomplished the mission assigned to the regiment with honour.

Especially distinguishing themselves in the battles against the Chinese invaders were Battalion Cmdr. LTC Smirnov, Dep. Cmdr. for Pol. Affairs Major Gatin, acting Cmdr. of 4th MRC LT Bayutov, LT Khrapov, SGT Yarulin, SGT Nikonov, SGT Badmatov, and Privates Bogdanovich, Levin, Spitsyn, Shtoyko, Koltakov, Leskov, Abintazov, Yegorov, Shopin, Mamontov, Gorokhov, Bedarev, Kupytov, Pastukhov, and Gubenko.

Privates Gelvikh, Potapov, Orekhov,[14] Bedarev, Koltakov, Shtoyko, and Kuzmin died in the battles for the Motherland, during the liberation of Damansky Isl., exhibiting here exceptional bravery and heroism.

I order

1. I express my gratitude to all personnel of 2nd MRB for the bravery and heroism they exhibited in the battles against the Chinese invaders.

2. By 18:00 on 16 March, the commander of 2nd MRB will present a list of officers, sergeants, and enlisted men who distinguished themselves in the battles to liberate Damansky Isl. from the Chinese invaders, with combat profiles, for the presentation of government awards to them.

3. The order is to be communicated to all regimental personnel.

Eternal glory to the heroes who fell in battles for the Motherland.
Commander: COL Krupeynikov
Chief of Staff: LTC Stepanov

This is what the official description of what happened looked like (below is quoted the text of Order No. 286, dated 19 November 1969, signed by Marshal of the Soviet Union M.V. Zakharov, deputy minister of defence of the USSR):

Junior Sergeant V.V. Orekhov, machine-gunner of 5th Company of military unit 35236, demonstrated a model of bravery and dedicated execution of his military duty in battles for the defence of the sacred borders of the Soviet state.

In March 1969, Junior Sergeant Orekhov, as part of his subunit, took part in battles against violators of the border of the Soviet Union, who provocatively attacked Soviet border units. With machine gun in hand, Junior Sergeant Orekhov advanced in the company line. With accurate fire from his machine gun, he destroyed a machine-gun team, inflicted considerable casualties, and then put to flight a large group of enemy soldiers, who were trying to execute a flank strike against the company. Although wounded, Junior Sergeant Orekhov did not leave the battlefield, but rather continued to advance together with his comrades. After being wounded a second time, he still remained in formation.

Overcoming his pain, he continued to support the actions of his company with machine-gun fire, and inflicted major casualties on the enemy. With his personal example of bravery, the courageous machine-gunner inspired the company soldiers to valiantly fight the enemy. In this battle, Junior Sergeant Orekhov, carrying out his military duty to the end, died the death of the valiant for our socialist Motherland.

By order of the Presidium of the Supreme Soviet of the USSR, dated 31 July 1969,[15] Sergeant V.V. Orekhov is posthumously awarded the Hero of the Soviet Union

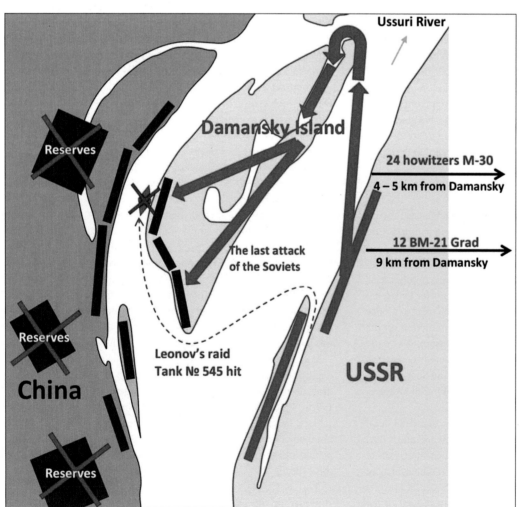

Sketch Map 4. The end of the battle on 15 March 1969 (after 17:00 local time). (Map by authors)

medal for bravery and heroism exhibited in the defence of the USSR State border.

His wholehearted loyalty to the socialist Motherland and fidelity to his military oath should serve as an example for all servicemen of the Armed Forces of the USSR.

I order that:

Hero of the Soviet Union Junior Sergeant Vladimir Viktorovich Orekhov be enrolled forever in the lists of 5th Company of military unit 35236. The order is to be communicated to personnel.[16]

A.D. Konstantinov, one of the veterans of the battle, recalled that Orekhov acted exceptionally calmly, and his accurate fire did, indeed, inflict considerable losses on the enemy. However, at some moment in the battle, for some reason he stood all the way up, and at this moment he was cut down by a machine-gun burst. Another veteran said that after this Orekhov was still alive, and crawled more than 100 metres to his own men.[17]

Sporadic crossfire erupted in the Damansky region even after 15 March. Soon after the ice on the Ussuri began to melt, and it became difficult to conduct combat operations.

M. I. Koleshnya recalled:

A decision was made to secure the island with the help of fire cover. Several heavy machine guns were set up on our side, at the tops of high hills; border details with machine guns and sniper rifles were positioned in trenches on our riverbank, opposite Damansky and Kirkinsky Islands. Each time, as soon as the violators attempted to land on the islands, they were immediately fired upon. It is difficult to judge how effective the firing was, because the trees and shrubbery had already turned green, and it was impossible to shoot accurately.[18]

A description of the battle by members of the Chinese General Staff is of definite interest. The following is the text of their note to the Communist Party of China (CPC) leadership:

The second battle on Zhenbao Island happened on 15 March. The Soviet troops were supported by larger numbers of tanks, armoured vehicles, and heavy-calibre guns. They put one motorised infantry battalion, one tank battalion, and four heavy-artillery battalions into the battle. However, our soldiers, following Chairman Mao's teaching that we should "fight no battle unless victory is sure," had made sufficient preparations in advance. On the night before, our soldiers landed on the island and laid out anti-tank mines. On the morning of the 15th, when the enemy dispatched to the island six armoured vehicles and more than 30 soldiers, we also transferred more troops there. At 8:02 a.m., the enemy launched the first attack. After one-hour's fierce fighting, we destroyed two enemy armoured vehicles. The remnants of the enemy escaped to the bank of their side of the river. At 9:40 a.m., the enemy launched the second wave of attack with the support of covering fire. Our soldiers dealt with the attack calmly by concentrating their firing on the enemy's tanks and armoured vehicles. They destroyed two enemy tanks and two armoured vehicles, and damaged another [armoured vehicle]. Two hours later the enemy's attack was completely repulsed. Beginning at 1:35 p.m., the enemy used heavy-calibre artillery, as well as tank and armoured vehicle guns, to shell our positions for two hours. At 3:13 p.m., they dispatched ten tanks, 14 armoured vehicles, and over 100 infantry soldiers to launch another attack

on Zhenbao Island. Our soldiers on the island. … waited for them to get close and then suddenly opened fire on them. … Our artillery units on the [Chinese] bank also took the opportunity to strike at the enemy, destroying one enemy tank and four armoured vehicles, and damaged two armoured vehicles. Then our artillery units continued to shell the enemy's border patrol stations and bunkers, killing a colonel and a lieutenant colonel. The enemy's casualties are estimated to be over 60. In addition, the enemy has lost two tanks and seven armoured vehicles, with another two tanks and four armoured vehicles being damaged.[19]

Thus, the Chinese version of the events is again a capricious mixture of truth, lies, a very accurate chronology, and typical propaganda.

On 15 March, General Chen Xilian, Commander of Shenyang Military District (see Vol. 1), was in Peking and in continuous communication with PLA commanders at the scene of events. The following is his description of the battle:

After the battle on 2 March, we were fully aware that the enemy would try to come back again, therefore we laid large numbers of mines at the promontory of the [Ussuri] river [bank]. [When the battle began on 15 March], a Soviet tank coming from the west was quickly blown up by us. They did not dare to come from the same direction [again]. Covered by supporting artillery fire, they dispatched more than thirty soldiers to launch an attack on the front. At that time, we did not deploy any troops on the [Zhenbao] island, but our artillery forces were ready to shell the enemy. Onto the small island with a size less than one square kilometre, the enemy dispatched dozens of trucks and other vehicles, and a dozen tanks and armoured vehicles. I asked Premier Zhou Enlai whether or not we should open fire. After the Premier said "yes", I immediately ordered our troops to open fire. The firing lasted for about thirty minutes, turning Zhenbao Island into a sea of flame. The enemy's trucks, tanks and armoured vehicles were all destroyed. They did not send more troops to the island but began using artillery forces to shell us. Our artillery forces also shelled them. After a while that day's battle ended.[20]

Here the battle is presented in a completely distorted way, and the truth can barely be glimpsed through the pile of lies.

Some contemporary Russian authors also think it possible to paint the 15 March events by attaching to them the character of a Hollywood war movie. For example, this is what one can read about the 15 March battle in a solid publication such as *Kommersant-Vlast*:

At around one o'clock hundreds of border guards contained the onslaught of several thousand. …

The ground was blood-soaked. …

And when not a single border guard remained on the island and the exultant Chinese had filled the island, the "Grads" began to talk. …

When, having replenished their ammunition, the soldiers of the motorised manoeuvre detachment returned to the island, they saw hell. Hundreds of burned, torn, and swept-up bodies.

Our artillery. … was pounding the Chinese riverbank. The ice along it had turned into a bloody mess,[21] but the Chinese had lugged boards and mats and floated on them with insane stubbornness to the island. Shells drowned them in bunches, but the officers shot those who hesitated, and the crazed Chinese jumped into the icy Ussuri water.[22]

Yes, the description of the battle looks sound. There is one problem: there is not a word of truth here. Furthermore, the title of the article – 'From the History of a Great Friendship' – leaves a rather unpleasant impression, inasmuch as it contains the kind of sarcasm that is so widespread in today's Russian mass media. Is this a case, however, when sarcasm is appropriate?

Infamous author Eduard Limonov also made a personal contribution to the distortion of the history of the war on the Ussuri River. Sitting on a bunk in cell No. 24 in the pre-trial detention centre at Lefortovo, Limonov wrote an article about the reasons for the Russian's eternal apathy. Walking round, he noted: 'Living waves of Chinese soldiers charged across Damansky Island, and they were fried by flamethrowers. But the authorities hid the heroes. However, those who should have sung the praises of the heroes didn't know how to, even if they had been allowed to.'[23] From whom did he hear about any flamethrowers? Why are these fables circulated – is there really not enough truthful information to tell about the real circumstances of the battle?

Obviously, authors of the urban myths about the Soviets using lasers, volumetric explosion bombs, and other miracle weapons belong to this same category of irresponsible fantasists. We have heard about piles of atomic weapons allegedly brought by the Soviet troops to the island – there is no need to comment about this delusion.

American historian Thomas Robinson, acknowledged in the West as the chief expert on issues of the Sino-Soviet border war, did not write about the 15 March battle in great detail, and so he is somewhat confused. He made a number of mistakes, which are completely explainable by the lack of information:

The battle on the 15th was somewhat different than that of the 2d. Preparations on both sides were much more complete, forces were much larger, losses were higher, and the engagement lasted much longer. There was also no element of surprise. In contrast to the encounter on March 2, it is not clear who began the battle on the 15th: Soviet and Chinese sources differ, of course, and the Soviet documentation is again much more voluminous. This time the Russian case is much less convincing, and the moral overtone present in reports of the earlier battle is muted, if not entirely absent. Both sides probably had built up their forces in the intervening fortnight, intending to wrest permanent control of the island away from the other or, failing that, to deny the other side its unhindered use.

Although initial reports seem somewhat vague, apparently the Russians increased the frequency of their patrols of the island after March 2. They still did not station a permanent force on the island, however, lest the Chinese zero in on them with artillery and mortar. A small scouting party did spend the night of the 14–15th on the island, and it is possible that this group was used as bait to lure the Chinese into a frontal attack. The Chinese say that the other side sent "many" tanks to the island and the river-arm ice about 4:00 a.m. on the 15th, attacking Chinese guards on patrol. It is not clear why such a large force would be needed to attack a patrol.[24]

This excerpt contains a curious sentence: Robinson says that on the night of 15 March the Soviet detachment on Damansky (that is, Yanshin's group) played the role of a kind of bait. The Soviet command ostensibly attempted in this way to force the Chinese to attack. It is difficult to confirm or reject this statement; however, Soviet veterans regard the orders at that time from their superiors,

first to leave the island, then to occupy it again, as an indication of uncertainty. It seems that they are right, because if there had been some clever plan, the Chinese, executing a frontal attack, should have been subjected to mass shelling, but they were not.

The Soviets state that their own early-morning patrol, consisting of two armored cars led by Senior Lieutenant Lev Mankovsky, discovered a group of Chinese lodged on the island, who had apparently sneaked over the previous night. Whatever the initial cause, the battle began in earnest around 9:45 or 10:00 a.m., with mortar and artillery fire from the Chinese bank and, by 10:30, according to Soviet accounts, heavy fire from three points on the Chinese bank.

The Chinese now threw more than a regiment (around 2000 men) of infantry into the fray, charging across the ice and gaining possession of at least part of the island. The Russians, when they saw this wave of Chinese, sought to block their advance with fire from machine guns mounted on armored personnel carriers, but moved back, either entirely off the island or to its eastern extremity, when they saw that the Chinese had a clear superiority in men. (Russian accounts speak of a ratio of ten Chinese to every Russian.) The Chinese directed intense artillery fire not only at the Soviet troops but also at the eastern channel of the river separating the island from the Soviet bank, evidently in the hope of slowing or stopping the movement of heavy vehicles over the ice. The Russians, adopting American Korean War tactics, allowed the Chinese to advance, and then counterattacked with large numbers of tanks, armored cars, and infantry in armored personnel carriers. Soviet artillery, brought in since the March 2 incident, launched a fierce barrage at 1:00 p.m., raking Chinese positions as far inland as 4 miles.[25]

Robinson's suggestion that Soviet troops used some American tactics cannot be taken seriously. By this time the Soviet Army had such a large amount of experience, that there were no secrets for it in the field of combined arms battle tactics. In addition, the depth of shelling of Chinese territory indicated here (four miles) is somewhat exaggerated. Nor was the stated time that the Soviets opened fire accurate.

Three such attacks were launched, each breaking through the Chinese positions. The first two faltered when ammunition was expended. The third apparently broke the Chinese position on the island, and the Chinese retreated to their own bank, taking their dead and wounded. The Soviets state that they did not follow up the Chinese retreat with large-scale garrisoning of the island, although they continued intense patrolling. The battle was over at 7:00 p.m., having lasted more than nine hours. Sources state that the Russians lost about 60 men (including the border post commander, Colonel D.V. Leonov) and the Chinese 800. (The number of Soviet casualties was lower probably because the Soviets had an advantage in tactics and armament.)[26]

The last statement is only partly true, inasmuch as Soviet superiority in weapons boiled down to the strike by rocket launchers, which surprised the Chinese (Robinson simply did not know about them, and, therefore, did not mention them). The participation of tanks and APCs in the battle compensated for the large number of Chinese guns and mortars and antitank grenade launchers.

Robinson does not report where he obtained the casualty figures for the sides: the term 'sources' that he uses allows for too many versions. However, the more than thirteen-fold difference in casualties seemingly strongly perplexes the American scholar. In a footnote he adds: 'The breakdown between dead and wounded is not clear in the statistics of either side. Surely the Chinese figure, even if accurate, represents both dead and wounded.'[27] Here, the lack of information lets Robinson down: he does not know that

on 15 March the Soviets used salvo fire systems and area firing. He also does not know that the 'Grad' salvo landed not on the infantry concentrated in trenches, but on the Chinese reserves gathered on small sectors of the riverbank.

In any case, the theme of Chinese casualties merits separate consideration.

2
TANK NO. 545

There is still no good explanation as to why Colonel D.V. Leonov was moving in tanks in the channel.

If by his manoeuvre he wanted to thwart the expected Chinese attack in the direction of the southern end of the island, then they should have struck the clustering enemy infantry from tank cannons and machine guns. This, however, was not done, although each tank was fully armed.

If, however, the task was to cut off contact between the Chinese riverbank and PLA subunits fighting on the island, then, again, they should have used tank weapons. This also, however, was not done.

It is difficult to explain this as a possible intention on the part of Leonov to capture a Chinese prisoner, inasmuch as such an act is not done in tanks. As was said earlier, it was as if some high-ranking person by phone blamed Leonov that the battle had been underway for several hours already, but the border guards had not yet been able to take a prisoner.

It seems that the decision was made hastily, without the necessary assessment of the situation that had developed. However, Leonov was not to blame for this. A very serious psychological situation had developed for him, as the commander. After all, the colonel's subordinates had truly fought and died on the island, while a powerful force in the form of 135th MRD was standing in the rear and not doing anything. Apparently, that is when the always calm and mature Leonov decided to undertake something unexpected in order to reverse the course of the battle.

One of the eyewitnesses, V.P. Fateyev (former sergeant major of the Nizhne-Mikhaylovka Outpost), recalled how, in general, the idea

of using tanks came about: 'Leonov decided to use tanks to cut off access to the island for the Chinese. As I was told, he asked: "Tanks – how?" He was told: "Tanks are impenetrable. The T-62". ...'[1]

There are two versions of how Leonov's T-62 tank, hull No. 545, was hit. The first: the tank was struck by a hollow-charge grenade that had been fired from an RPG-2-type antitank grenade launcher. The second: the tank blew up on a Chinese mine.

The majority of Soviet/Russian authors hold to the first version. However, it should be taken into consideration that the distance from the tank to the Chinese riverbank was around 150 metres, that is, at the limit of the range of fire of an RPG-2. Therefore, a shot from the Chinese bank of the Ussuri could hardly have destroyed a T-62. Moreover, it is known that the T-62's left caterpillar track was broken: in principle, a grenade from an RPG-2 can cause such damage, but how, then, can it be explained that the tank crew and Leonov were wounded at the moment the tank was struck? After all, in this case the energy of a hollow-charge jet would have been used up when the caterpillar track exploded, and not in penetrating the armour. Thus, the first version is very doubtful.

The second version has been advanced by some Chinese authors: having learned from the bitter experience of the 2 March events, the Chinese were worried that the Soviet APCs might have had a greater capability of moving between the island and the Chinese riverbank. For this purpose, on the night of 14–15 March, a PLA reconnaissance platoon laid antitank mines, packaged in white for camouflage, on the ice. The lead T-62 drove onto a mine and blew up. That being said, Chinese sources confirm the fact of the shelling of the tanks by

Leonov's damaged tank on the ice of the Ussuri River. (Chinese Internet)

RPG-2 grenade launchers. Moreover, a Chinese photo can be found on the Internet, which allegedly shows the hull of Leonov's tank with holes that resemble what a hollow-charge grenade would make. It is not certain, however, that this photo is of that particular tank.

To sum up, the following can be proposed. Upon the appearance of the tanks between the island and the Chinese riverbank, the Chinese began to fire from grenade launchers (which the Soviets had observed, since a grenade in flight leaves quite a visible fire trail). This shelling was ineffective, but when the tank drove onto the mine and an explosion followed, from the Soviet riverbank this was perceived as a grenade hit, and so the first version came about. It is possible, however, that firing continued from grenade launchers (not only from the Chinese riverbank, but also from the island) against the immobile tank, and one of the grenades reached its target.

Whatever version is, in the final analysis, the true one, there is no doubt about the result: the T-62 was stopped and turned into an immobile sitting duck.

Colonel Leonov ordered the crew to leave the vehicle, after which they got out through the escape hatch, located on the bottom of the tank. Leonov himself had been wounded in the soft tissue of his legs. Nevertheless, he was also able to get out of the tank. At that very moment a ricocheting bullet struck him down. To be more precise, it was not even the bullet, but rather its casing.

The tank crew was able to make its way across the island to Yanshin's group, after which Junior Lieutenant Dergachev, the tank platoon leader, reported about Leonov's death. To the question of why they had not pulled the colonel out, the tank crew answered vaguely and unintelligibly. Some researchers treat this fact as a manifestation of cowardice, but with a more detailed study a completely different explanation emerges.

The fact is that practically all crew members were wounded or shell-shocked. Nevertheless, the tankers were dragging away Private Kuzmin (at that moment, he was already dead, but in the confusion of the battle no one noticed this, and everyone thought that he was only wounded). As for Leonov, the crew saw him die, and, therefore, nothing could be done to help the colonel. They had no energy to carry off the body of the dead man. To this can be added the thunder of battle, the abrupt change in the situation, and general stress. In general, it is clearly premature to accuse the tank crew of cowardice.

The episode with the destruction of tank No. 545 had already become surrounded by unsubstantiated rumours in March 1969, and now, decades later, the event is still sometimes distorted beyond recognition. For example, V. Fridyev, a journalist from Primorsky Radio who was at the scene of the battle, still wrote the following many years after the events:

The violators were crushed by machine-gun fire from the rear in the channel between the island and the Chinese riverbank. All types of weapons fired against the tank, but unsuccessfully. And suddenly a Chinese soldier with a handheld grenade launcher jumped out from the bushes, and from about ten metres away planted a grenade in the reserve fuel tank (there were 4 of them on armour, with 200 litres of diesel fuel in each). Almost a ton of fuel blazed the sky, engulfing the tank in a fiery blanket. From our riverbank we saw how an enormous tongue of flame, wrapped in smoke, leapt up like a funeral banner behind the island.[2]

Several mistakes are immediately apparent in this brief excerpt. Leonov did not crush the violators with machine-gun fire, a Chinese soldier did not jump out from the bushes, and there were not tons of fuel on the tank. A little earlier this same author stated that on Leonov's order cannon ammunition was unloaded from the tank, and the crew had no loader. Neither is true. And for some reason this author mentioned only Leonov's tank, but said nothing about the other three vehicles.

On the night of 16 March, three reconnaissance and search groups – two from 135th MRD (headed by Reconnaissance Company Commander Mikhail Barkovsky) and one from the border guards (headed by Senior Lieutenant N.I. Nazarenko) – were sent to the island. It was Nazarenko who discovered the dead chief of the Iman Border Detachment. Yu. Babansky, who also took part in the search, helped to carry the colonel's body away.

Information about how specifically Private Aleksey Kuzmin, the loader, died appeared in 1969. Unfortunately, it was not without the regular fantasies:

The combat vehicle on which Colonel D. Leonov, the battle commander, rode arrived in the rear of the Maoists. And suddenly a shell fell on board. Shrapnel wounded the colonel. The vehicle had to be abandoned.

"Lesha," comrades said to Kuzmin, "help get the colonel out through the hatch. And go to the rear yourself. You're wounded, after all."

But Aleksey did not leave his comrades. Together with them he transferred to another armoured personnel carrier and fought from there. When this vehicle also caught fire, he continued to advance on foot.[3]

Funeral of Colonel D.V. Leonov in Iman, 20 March 1969. From right to left: widow, daughter, mother. (from V.N. Volik)

Tank No. 545 on the Chinese riverbank. (Military Museum of Hanoi, via Albert Grandolini)

Once again it should be repeated: Aleksey Kuzmin, in fact, died not far from the tank, as he was withdrawing with his comrades to his own side. He was awarded the Order of the Red Banner (posthumously) for his participation in the battle.

Witnesses to the events say that the first attempt to tow the tank to Soviet territory was undertaken on 17 March. On this day a special recovery group, including three tanks and two tractors, was sent for the T-62. The Chinese immediately perceived what would now follow, and they opened defensive fire from guns and mortars. From the Soviet riverbank artillery also responded, and rather accurately. All three of the artillery regiment's battalions, a 130mm cannon battalion (which had arrived in the Damansky area on 16 March), and 'Grad' rocket launchers conducted fire. In particular, the artillery regiment's 3rd Battalion (7th and 8th artillery batteries), equipped with 152mm D-1 howitzers, received the task of suppressing the Chinese ISU-122 self-propelled assault gun battery. This battery (four vehicles) had advanced from the ice in the direction of Damansky, apparently for the purpose of conducting direct laying fire against the recovery group. As a result of the battalion fire, one Chinese assault gun blew up, another caught fire, and the two remaining vehicles took cover in the forest. The fire along the Chinese riverbank on 17 March was so dense, that the commander of the 3rd Battalion ordered that fire be conducted in salvos against the assault gun batteries, in order to identify the explosions of the battalion's shells in the general mass of fire.

During the 17 March battle, a considerable portion of the Chinese fire resources was suppressed; however, the Soviets did not succeed in towing tank No. 545 to their side. The fact is that in attempting to throw a tow rope onto the damaged vehicle, Junior Sergeant A.I. Vlasov, a tanker from 5th Tank Company, died, and one other soldier was wounded. The comrades dragged off the body of the dead man; however, the operation was squelched and the tank remained on the Ussuri ice.

By the way, an observer of the events spoke about the attempt to tow the tank across the island, for which a special tractor was brought to Damansky. This statement should also be acknowledged to be either a mistake or a misunderstanding: the height of the western bank of Damansky was so great that this method of recovery was probably rejected during the discussion stage (if such an idea was even put forth).

Meanwhile, Mao's soldiers exhibited great efficiency, having managed during the dark part of the day to remove a secret device for stabilising cannons and night-vision instruments.

Inasmuch as the recovery of the tank was admitted to be undoable, the Soviet command decided to destroy Leonov's T-62 by detonation. There were two explosions, and both were unsuccessful: at first, too few explosives were laid and the vehicle was undamaged; then this mistake was corrected, but the powerful explosion only threw the tank into the air. Let us mention: both times the explosives were placed under the tank. No one, even today, can explain why charges were not put inside the tank.

New attempts to blow up the tank were not crowned with success: the Chinese immediately opened fire, and this threatened to result in new victims. And strict instructions came from Moscow: do not allow the death of one more man. The decision was then made to use mortars.

Firing from 240mm mortars, particularly those brought from Ussuriysk, was unsuccessful. Some witnesses said that it was as if Leonov's vehicle had become invulnerable: mortar bombs fell on the right and on the left, in front of and behind it, but in no way did they achieve their goal. To put it briefly, they did not fall into the tank; the ice then broke and the T-62 vanished from sight. The Chinese took advantage of this circumstance and for a month and a half they prepared to raise the tank from the bottom of the river (to do this, a group of divers from one of the PRC naval bases and four tractors were brought in). Finally, during the first days of May, the T-62 turned up on that riverbank. In addition to the vehicle, the Chinese got a new 115mm smoothbore tank cannon and ammunition for it, and an engine.

Some Chinese sources shed light on how the PLA soldiers managed to bring up the Soviet tank (naturally, one should treat such information with a good measure of caution). In particular, they said that the work was not done during the day, inasmuch as the Chinese feared a fire strike from the Soviet riverbank. The divers also did not work at night, because the night-vision instruments that the border guards had made it possible to record activity taking place in darkness. The divers dived only during the brief period of dusk, when the sun setting in the west made observation difficult for the Soviets. The precautions turned out to be a good idea: the Chinese say that it was namely at this time that Soviet snipers killed one of the work leaders, Deputy Commander of 77th Division Sun

The Chinese hold a rally at the captured tank No. 545. (Chinese Internet)

Tank No. 545 in the Military Museum, Beijing. (Chinese Internet)

Zhengmin (according to other information, he held the post of Deputy Commander of Engineer Units of the Shenyang Military District, and he died when he was blown up by a mine). These same Chinese sources said that each diver worked underwater no more than 15 minutes (because of the cold).

Now, when so many years after the events in the Ussuri have passed, it is not so simple to answer whether the T-62 could have been retrieved, rather than surrendering it to the Chinese.

The recollections of veterans make it possible, all the same, to answer this question in the affirmative. After all, the tank was located on Soviet territory, and all the work of the Chinese to extract it from the bottom of the river was accompanied by constant border violations. If the Soviet command had rigorously reacted to this and had not hesitated to use its available combat equipment, then the Chinese would not have been able to do anything. However, Moscow had decided to end the conflict as soon as possible, even at the cost of losing a secret tank.

During the 15 March battle, there was one moment when the recovery of the damaged vehicle could have been done quickly and without casualties, with the help of another tank – immediately after the 'Grad' salvos and the following victorious attack of the border guards and the motorised riflemen. They did not figure this out. …

A recent ridiculous suggestion is associated with the loss of T-62 No. 545. 'Experts' were found who, in general, reduce the entire conflict on Damansky down to a struggle for this very tank.

Allegedly there were many secrets in it, and because of this the battle unfolded. Strictly speaking, there is nothing in particular to refute here: the incongruities with the elementary logic of authors of such 'discoveries' are obvious for anyone who is more or less familiar with the reasons and course of the conflict. Finally, knowing the Chinese passion for copying anything and everything, it is logical to ask the question: did they then produce something similar to the T-62 or not?

Internet enthusiasts will most easily find the answer: it is enough for them to search using the key phrase 'WZ-122 basic Chinese combat tank.' The universal network will obligingly provide a photograph in which the twin of the T-62 is presented. As they say, find at least a couple of differences.

Leonov's tank No. 545 is now in the Beijing Military Museum.

3

THE EVENTS OF 15 AND 17 MARCH THROUGH THE EYES OF VETERANS

Letters of veterans make it possible to find out many interesting details about what happened on Damansky Island on 15 and 17 March 1969.[1] Of course, there may be errors in these recollections, but, in any case, this is documented evidence from eyewitnesses who did not and do not have any personal interest in distorting the actual picture of the battle.

Nikolay Ivanovich Popov recalls the following:[2]

On the night of 14-15 March, at 23:30, I was summoned to see Chief of the Detachment Colonel D.V. Leonov. In addition to me, Lieutenant Colonel Ye.I. Yanshin, Senior Lieutenant V.I. Solovyev, Senior Lieutenant L.K. Mankovsky, and Lieutenant A.F. Klyga arrived to receive the tasks (although, strictly speaking, at first we did not know why we had been asked to come). The situation was reported to us, and a conclusion was made about Chinese capabilities and new provocations coming from their side. The task was assigned for a group of border guards to move to Damansky Island on four 60PB APCs, and, if there were any Chinese there, to drive them away (on 14 March the details had been removed from the island). If there were none there, then we were to situate ourselves on the island and set up a defence near the southern part, in the area of the rampart. At 1:30 I began to move with my group from the Nizhne-Mikhaylovka Outpost in the direction of the island (we left all together in a column).

We formed up before embarking, Lieutenant Colonel A.D. Konstantinov said a few parting words, and then, when everyone had boarded the APCs (I was in my APC No. 2), he walked up and said: "Watch out, Popov, I need all of you alive."

We took a lot of ammunition and grenades (all this came in handy later). Thus, each officer had 10 men (a total of 40 men), and there were five of us officers (Lieutenant Colonel Yanshin was the senior man). A total of 45 men and 4 APCs.

Earlier, there had been no road, as such, there simply was a path through the forest to the island. At 5:30 on 15 March, the groups approached the northern part of the island, and advanced across a small inlet from our side closer to the southern part of the island. My group (9 border guards and APC driver Smelov, i.e., 10 men) and Senior Lieutenant Mankovsky's group (10 men) set up at the end of a swamp, which was located near the beginning of the rampart, around 50 metres from one another, perhaps a bit more, and the gap between the groups was covered by APCs, which later could not continuously stay in place.

I gave the command to disperse along the swamp and prepare a trench for firing from a lying position, although there was nothing in particular to prepare it with – how can you pull that off with ice, a little snow and grass, and dry branches? The other two groups (Klyga's and Senior Lieutenant Solovyev's) set up behind us behind a bend in the swamp.

There were no Chinese on the island (no voices could be heard, no fires, nothing was even seen on the hills). We lay in our trenches, listened to the terrain, wanted to drink, but there was no water anyway; therefore, we used "Duchess" hard candies.

At dawn Lieutenant Colonel Yanshin sent Senior Lieutenant Mankovsky and four border guards to the southern part of the island to find out if there were any Chinese there. They returned a half hour later and reported that there were no Chinese. After dawn fully broke the Chinese turned on their loudspeaker and began their propaganda against us in Russian (apparently the tape had been recorded, because two versions of one and the same text were repeated several times).

The first: "Officers and soldiers of the Soviet Army, you have violated the border of the PRC, this is an armed provocation against the Chinese people. You must leave Chinese territory, otherwise you will be held responsible for what happens." And so forth.

The second was a long speech, which said that Damansky Island and other islands were Chinese. It ended with: "Down with the new tsars. Down with Brezhnev!"

At 9:30 on 15 March, Yanshin once again sent Mankovsky and four border guards to reconnoitre the southern end of the island. This time from our river bank (Krasnaya Hill) our vehicle broadcast in Chinese that Damansky and other islands were Soviet, and a reference was made to treaties that had been concluded earlier.

At 9:45 I heard a long automatic burst. This was the Chinese, who were advancing to the island, from behind their support rampart, which was located on the Chinese riverbank (apparently left behind by the Japanese); they had encountered our reconnaissance group and fired on it. About 10–15 minutes before this, some sentence (a command) was heard in a Chinese-language broadcast. Immediately after automatic fire from small arms, the Chinese opened heavy mortar and artillery fire from the hills along the island. Two groups (Solovyev's and Klyga's) fell under this fire; they were located behind us, but the moving barrage did not reach us, because the Chinese, operating by the "infiltration" method, had begun to fill up the southern part of the island and apparently feared getting caught by their own fire.

My group, since it was the most forward one, was the first to engage in the battle, then Mankovsky's group. A fire battle began. All four APCs began to fire from the turret machine guns, simultaneously manoeuvring so as not to fall into the field of fire. We fought this way for an hour and a half. We began to use up the ammunition (although we had taken a lot of it), and the Chinese began to actively press us. A decision was made to withdraw from the island (otherwise, it would have been the end of us); communications with the island had been severed because the Chinese had cut the APCs' whip antennas. While firing we began to board the APCs. Six men were already wounded, including two in my group (one in the arm, one in the leg). Senior Lieutenant Solovyev had suffered a contusion in the head during the artillery shelling. By some miracle I was still alive. A machine gunner, who had fired on my command, was next to me; we opened a case of F-1 grenades. I thought that now the Chinese would stumble onto the case – anyway, they had detected the place where the machine gunner and I were lying and had begun to conduct heavy fire against us. We had just changed place (we had crawled off to the side), when there was a long machine-gun burst and the Chinese ran toward us. My fur coat was new, the hem was in tatters, but I had not been hit. Yanshin saw this and brought over the APC; we crawled into the APC through the side hatch and then, firing through the embrasures, all four APCs left the island. All of my APC's wheels had been punctured, and it moved with difficulty (on the spit, as soon as the driver killed the engine, it turned over with all eight wheels onto the rim).

The wounded were handed over, forces began to regroup, and our reserves approached. Counterattacks against the island were organised, but they were unsuccessful, because the Chinese conducted a heavy artillery shelling along the river, and they occupied the southern part of the island. Once again we returned to our spit. Lieutenant Colonel Konstantinov assigned me the task: conduct fire using machine-gun and grenade-launcher teams along the channel and do not give new reserves the chance to cross over from the Chinese riverbank to the island, which we succeeded in doing, although this was not easy.

At around 13:00, three of our aircraft arrived, flew at different altitudes, and left. They did not conduct fire.

At around 14:00 it quieted down, and we began to have lunch (a field kitchen had arrived). The Chinese apparently saw us from the hills, and several mortars struck our spit. One bomb fell on top of an APC, another struck our SPG-9 team, and one border guard was blown up (his remains were laid in a bullet crate). We all ran off in different directions and went on the defensive. Other explosions did no damage, and there was no more firing.

We began again to eat our *kasha*, which I had never eaten, but hunger had taken its toll here. A T-62 tank company had arrived, and then Leonov, who had not received artillery fire support (although the army command had been asked for this several times) boarded one of the tanks; 3 tanks (with Leonov in the first) set off along V.D. Bubenin's 2 March route, firing from the rear and the flank. Once again the border guards and a motorised rifle company from 2nd Motorised Rifle Battalion, 199th Verkhne-Udinsky Regiment, set off from the spit, and battle ensued on the island once more.

Only at 17:00 did the artillery and "Grad" battalion strike the Chinese riverbank, channel, and hills, which decided the outcome of the battle. At first a mortar battery opened fire, then artillery, almost killing their own men, and Konstantinov had to make a racket on the phone for a long time in order to have the firing shifted further; artillery began to fire closer to the Chinese riverbank, along the channel, and along the Chinese spit.

Eight times during the day we took the island, then had to withdraw under Chinese fire. As for the combat and moral qualities of the Chinese soldiers, the main thing is that they were fanatics who would carry out an order at any cost, regardless of casualties, carrying off all dead and wounded. They adjusted fire from the trees very well.

After the shelling and suppression of the gunners, the Chinese ran off the island. My covering group worked exceptionally well, and we got rid of many Chinese (I fired from a machine gun, having had to personally rig the belts myself by hand). It was bad that there were no spare barrels, so it was necessary to detach the barrel and cool it down in the snow (a barrel had to be changed after 500 shots). Otherwise it overheated and firing would be ineffective. By 20:00 on 15 March, the Chinese had been completely driven off the island, and our sappers had mined the southern part of the island. After gathering everything that was necessary, I returned to the outpost at 1:30 (it was already 16 March).

Viktor Mikhaylovich Tirskikh served as signalman in the Iman Border Detachment. During the entire day on 15 March he provided communications and, therefore, knew what was happening. The following are his recollections:

I received the order to provide the company with communications in the conflict area. To provide the sergeant school and manoeuvre group with communications, a line of communications was forwarded to the island; it is true that after the latter left the Chinese got it all.

About the 15 March events. It was my shift. Of course, I have forgotten many details. Therefore, I will tell you only what I am sure of. No one demanded that Colonel D.V. Leonov take a prisoner – a "tongue" – I remember that precisely, because all that day I was working without a replacement, and I monitored all conversations with the district, the detachment commander's reports particularly attentively. Perhaps after 15 March someone got the idea that it would be good to exhibit a Chinese at a press conference, but on that day there was no talk about a prisoner. "At the top" there was no way they could make up their minds about the situation: what to do? how to proceed? Contradictory instructions were given. Therefore, Colonel Leonov ordered Major Dontsov (chief of the detachment's combat training) to record the time of all telephone instructions: who, what, and when. They would have to look for the right ones and the wrong ones. The situation reached a critical mass. The conversation was about using everything that the border detachment command had in reserve. Our signal company had a tracked APC equipped with a radio, but it did not have a single machine gun. Colonel Leonov decided to command from this tracked vehicle. And at this very moment a tanker turned to Leonov and suggested that the T-62 be used as the command vehicle. The tanks had only armour-piercing shells as its ammunition (soldier information), and for the destruction of enemy personnel – a machine gun and tracked vehicles.

If Aleksandr Dmitriyevich Konstantinov raked the 135th MRD leadership over the coals for its passivity, then I, from my narrow point of view, have to say that it seems to me that the start-up and maintenance of communications were done poorly.

The BM-21 "Grad" battalion fired a volley. Several minutes before this, General Major Nesov spoke on the telephone with General Lieutenant Rzhechitsky. They discussed the situation that had developed at this time. I knew these Soviet Army commanders, because they called Leonov quite often. They were hunters, and hunting in the border zone was their one pleasure; wild game in the area was not afraid of hunters. … For me, they were the greatest commanders in the Soviet Army – corps and division. With respect to the operational situation, I knew Admiral Ushakov, Captain 1st Rank Shkolnik, and our reliable assistants – the maritime units of the border guards. And at this moment Khabarovsk came on my line and asked: "Give me the command post. General Losik." For me, nothing could be more important than Vladivostok ("Albatross" was the call sign for our Primorsky Border District). Therefore, to the request that I give them the command post, I answered that the line was busy and I couldn't disconnect it, because I had two generals on the line. After hearing the refusal, he repeated his demand with a sterner tone of voice, which was imprinted in my memory for a long time: "Kid, if you don't want to start working in a disciplinary battalion, then quickly get me the command post; General Losik personally needs it." What struck me at that moment was the speed with which the two generals stopped talking after I broke into their conversation with my report. Curiosity pushed me to find out why General Losik needed the line, and just who he was. Naturally, the general himself wasn't speaking, most likely his deputy, who read the order about opening fire and firing a volley from the "Grad" grenade launcher. Later I found out that it was General of the Army O.A. Losik, Commander of the Far Eastern Military District, who demanded the line.

This order should be in the archives. There was never a question in my mind who gave the order. It was General O.A. Losik.

135th MRD continuously "hung" on the border detachment's line. This was both during the first days of its deployment and afterwards. "Hit them this way, good. They ran off. I don't see, they hid behind a hill. …" Therefore, I had the opportunity to be in the know about their problems for an extended period time. For a long time they discussed the problem with the tank, and after unsuccessful attempts to pull it out from the ice, and that by this time the Chinese basically had control of it, and the decision was made to sink it. They decided to use heavy mortars for this. I remember the arguments the officers made in support of this decision. "The tank will get sucked into the silt; you won't pull the damn thing out of the river. Remember, in exercises, when a tank got stuck in the mud, how the cables ripped … ." And once again Lieutenant Colonel Borisenko used our communications to correct fire.

After Borisenko's unit was removed from the border, Detachment Commander Colonel P.A. Alekseyev ordered that machine-gun positions (Vladimirov heavy machine guns) be outfitted on Kafyla Hill ("Rosa-1," "Rosa-2," and "Rosa-3") to oppose the Chinese in their attempts to extract the tank. They opened fire as soon as the Chinese began to "show signs of life" in the area of the sunken tank. A raft appeared, from which the divers were working. Actually, after they dismantled the cannon from the tank and chained it with a cable, the raft disappeared. Tractors like our S-100 were used, which, like barge haulers, tried almost every night to pull out the tank. In reply, our side turned on spotlights, and the machine-gun positions opened fire. The Chinese had outfitted shelters and trenches in case of gunfire. I remember reports by commanders about how many rounds were fired in the direction of the tank: 157, 120, 160. The next day there was a call from the district: "Colonel, what do you think you're doing? The Chinese have sent another note. Moscow is displeased. You are shelling their village of Hunzy and lighting up the territory. Stop." To which Colonel Alekseyev answered that our task was to prevent the tank from being taken. And the order followed: do not spare any rounds, do not allow the tank to be taken. Unfortunately, however, on the night of 1–2 May the tank was extracted from the silt and mud of the river channel with the help of tractors; the observation post reported this to the detachment's duty officer. The deep track left by the tank on the damp ground confirmed this report.

In March 1969, Nikolay Antonovich Zadorozhny occupied the post of chief of staff of 135th MRD's Rocket Forces and Artillery. On 15 and 17 March he was at the division's observation post; therefore, all events of these days passed before his very eyes. His excellent memory has retained many curious details about the events:

On 15 March, no one personally issued us an order to open fire along the Chinese riverbank. We received all orders from our immediate superiors by telephone. Our headquarters was located under Mount Kafyla, the observation post [NP] was on Mount Kafyla itself, and the division command post (where representatives of the corps and the district were located) was at the Nizhne-Mikhaylovka Outpost. The chief of the division's rocket forces and artillery (RViA) and I were continuously located at the NP, where there was telephone communication with division headquarters, and from 16 March – with district headquarters and Moscow (with secret communications device).

By 10:00 on 15 March, artillery was at the fire positions and the commanders were at the NP. We had to observe, and we regretted that we could not help the border guards who were fighting, because there was an order not to open fire without permission.

By 16:30 on 15 March, an order had been received by telephone: "At 17:00 Smirnov's battalion is to attack. Support the battalion attack with a ten-minute artillery strike along the island's western riverbank, but so that not a single shell explodes on the Chinese riverbank." We consulted with the chief of the RViA division, and he answered: "We cannot execute the task, remove the restrictions."

The fact is that the dispersion of shells for rocket artillery with respect to range is great: in the case of Damansky, it was approximately 500 metres for an overshot and the same for a shot that fell short (the width of the island itself was all of 500 metres). So there was no certainty whatsoever that shells would not explode on the Chinese riverbank. In fact, there was a high probability that our own men would be hit.

At 16:45 a new command arrived: "Open fire along the western riverbank and channel." Colonel Grigory Vlasovich Pentsak, chief of the division RViA, asked: "Open fire on your command or at a specific time?" The answer: "At a specific time." Which we did, firing one gun from each battery, making sure that not a single shell exploded over our men.

As for the restrictions, I don't know if they were generally removed.

On 17 March 1969, a recovery group was sent to the island. At that time General Lieutenant P.M. Plotnikov was at the NP. After the group had gone up to tank No. 545 and had begun to unwind the towing cable, the Chinese opened heavy fire. As a result, Junior Sergeant Vlasov died and his assistant was wounded.

The leader of the recovery group asked for help. General Plotnikov ordered: "Comrade Pentsak, suppress the enemy's fire resources." I think anyone else in his place would have acted the same. We carried out the general's order with great accuracy, because we could see all the Chinese positions, and all targets were distributed between the batteries and the battalions.

However, it is also true that 5–6 minutes later, when he saw the explosions on the Chinese riverbank, Plotnikov gave the order to cease firing. Of course, the ceasefire did not contribute to the recovery group's execution of its task.

Generally speaking, Leonov's tank could have been recovered. But the enemy had to be suppressed on his riverbank. Of course, this could have caused an escalation of the conflict; however, without artillery we once again would have lost the valuable lives of young soldiers.

No one wanted to take on the responsibility for firing along the Chinese riverbank. Even after our 16 March report that since morning the Chinese had taken the radio and shells from the tank and carried them off to their riverbank, no reply followed. Only about two hours later did a command come to not allow the Chinese to approach the tank. This meant that all these issues were decided in Moscow.

Nothing came of the 240mm mortar. I myself went up in a helicopter to correct fire. Then we brought concrete-piercing shells to the 152mm howitzer, and a direct hit levelled the turret; then the tank sank.

As for Chinese casualties on 15 March, I assume that no one, except for the Chinese themselves, knows their numbers. I think that the casualties were high. By our estimates, somewhere around a battalion. Many of the wounded froze because the Chinese command and control had been disrupted, and there were freezing temperatures that day.

The quality of combat training for the Chinese was not high. On the other hand, they were quite stubborn and maintained strict discipline. Their artillerymen were not trained in the best way: for example, the Chinese 152mm cannon-howitzer battalion was located 6–7 kilometres from our riverbank, but their fire was very imprecise. At first we observed explosions of their shells along the crest of their hills, then along their own riverbank, and the next volley was fired across our heads.

The most memorable of all these events for me was the volley of the rocket battalion. Especially that moment when the sound of explosions could no longer be heard, and the ground and ice had already risen with smoke and flames.

My memory also holds other moments that are seemingly not directly associated with one another: the whistle of Chinese shells over my head (I thought: "I began my service as a seventeen-year-old guy in the Soviet Army with a war – am I really going to end my service in a war?!"). Or I remember a herd of wild goats running from the Chinese riverbank to ours. …

I recall the border guards coming out of the battle on the Ussuri's snowy river bed. They were walking, completely exhausted, and then they suddenly fell down. Then each one got up and continued further. One was still lying there – what a joy it was when he too got up!

Former artillery officer L.G. Kushnirenko recalls the following:

Summer and autumn of 1968 I conducted field exercises, occupying the post of senior officer of the battalion's 2nd battery. Major Antonov was the battalion commander and Captain Vlasenko was the political officer.

On 2 March 1969 we had field firing training, conducted by General Major Smyk, chief of 45th Army Corps' Rocket Forces and Artillery. The firing was conducted on a training range outside the village of Tamga. In the afternoon we were all taken off the exercises and we returned to the unit. They informed us that to the north, in the area of Damansky Island, the chief of the outpost, his deputy, and several border guards had been killed.

On the night of 14–15 March our battalion was raised on alert, and we, with our headlights turned off, moved in a column along the route to the Damansky region. The M-30 howitzers were towed by AT-L light tractors. MT-LB tractors came soon after, before these events, and stood in reserve. However, with the permission of Battalion Commander Major Antonov, the second battery's driver–mechanic started up four of them and set off with us: one was at the disposal of the battalion commander, another was with the battery commander, and the other two were with the second battery's fire platoons.

On 15 March, the artillery regiment's top loader met us and pointed out the area of the fire positions. We occupied the positions and oriented our guns to the west, from where the thunder of guns and machine guns reached us.

My position was in a swamp with large hillocks, which had to be cut down. The mounts were reinforced with iron stakes. With us was the transportable ammunition, which we began to prepare for firing – cleaning off the grease, etc. Sometime during the second half of the day I received the command to open defensive fire, not in volleys, but rather methodically, one shot per gun. After that the correction was made to fire a volley, continuously increasing the sight setting. It turned out to be like conducting a moving barrage.

Fire was conducted against targets on the island itself, approaching the Chinese riverbank. We did not, however, fire into Chinese territory.

The conditions for conducting fire were very difficult: we did not sleep at night, there was no food (the kitchens had flipped over and had been thrown into a ditch by the armoured vehicles that were following them). Battery Sergeant Major Us and I divided the contents of my emergency bag, and we did the same thing with the food from Lieutenant Lyubchenko's (the 2nd fire platoon leader) bag – generally speaking, we somehow kept up the strength of the soldiers.

The swamp was covered with ice, and with each shot the gun was ripped out of its mount and turned on its side. Each time all personnel had to set it up again. And after all, the teams were only 50% manned: we needed 7 men, but there were only 3–4.

We shot at full charge. The soldiers worked like a single, well-coordinated mechanism, helping one another. They understood me at a single glance. And still the battalion commander rebuked us for not sustaining the rate of fire, although almost all the transportable ammunition had been used up. We did not touch the battalion reserve.

On the night of 15–16 March, we were moved to a new place. This was a level clearing near a small forest. All night we were busy with laying, adjusting, and surveying the fire position, and with monitoring the regimental surveying group. A report came that Colonel Leonov, Chief of the Border Detachment, and many other border guards had been killed. They brought to the position food and some vehicles with ammunition from the division reserve. They were unloaded, and stockpiles were formed near each gun.

16 March was Election Day. Captain Vlasenko, the battalion political officer, came and organised voting at each gun. Automatic firing could be heard periodically from the direction of the island.

On 17 March a recovery group, headed by Captain Kuzmin, advanced to the island to recover our damaged equipment and gather up the dead. A white flag with a red cross was waving on one of the tractors. The MT-LB tractor from our battery was part of this group. However, as the group approached Damansky Island, fire from Chinese territory was suddenly opened against it (the driver of the MT-LB told us about this later). At that moment I received the target by radio: "Suppress the mortar battery." This battery was firing against the recovery group and could be easily seen from the battalion commander's observation post.

A large column with personnel, headed by a general (I don't remember his name), stopped on the road near our fire position. The general walked up and asked about the situation. I reported that the target had been received – the mortar battery located on Chinese territory. To his question as to whether we needed help, I asked that shells be brought to the guns. This was immediately carried out.

We opened rapid fire. After the command "Stop! Cease firing," I was barely able to stop the firing, I had lost my voice. As the battalion commander later told us, only a black hole remained where the enemy mortar battery had been.

During the fire raid against Chinese territory, our artillery regiment's 2nd Battalion was firing from the right, and the rocket battalion was firing from the right and from behind. There was still the 130mm cannon battalion – somewhat behind.

After all this deafening racket, a literally tomb-like silence fell. For 3–4 days there generally was not a single shot.

We then shifted the fire position. The Chinese riverbank could be seen at the new place. Castling fire positions were determined 300 metres to the left and 300 metres to the right. A checkpoint with an MT-LB was set up on the road, with a continuous on-duty team, and a belt with rounds was loaded into the machine gun. Measures were taken to repel sabotage groups; there had been many reports about them. Near each gun a trench had been dug out in the frozen ground, and the ammunition was properly placed and camouflaged. The guns were also camouflaged with on-hand materials.

A female voice from the Chinese side could be heard through powerful speakers: "Get out of here!," "Nesov's gang – leave!," or "Vashchenko, Vashchenko, you don't have to fire a volley!" Sometime on 20–21 March, a vehicle with a special team and propaganda shells for the M-30 howitzer drove up to me at my fire position. Overnight we were supplied with leaflets rolled up

in tubes. When everything was ready, the command came to open fire along their territory – by grid and by gun. The command was satisfied with this firing.

I'd like to mention the actions of the battalion scouts, headed by Lieutenant Grigoryev. He was in charge of the group of scouts who protected the sappers: the latter were trying to destroy our damaged tank.

Two 240mm mortars and two D-1 howitzers were allocated to destroy this tank; they fired from half-direct laying. They discharged a large quantity of ammunition, but this firing did not produce the expected result.

At the end of March we were removed from the positions and sent by troop train to Pantaleymonovka, the place of our permanent deployment.

Anatoly Ivanovich Tsogla, a cadet in a training subunit in 1969, recalls the following:

They attached us students of a training subunit for preparing M-46 cannon team leaders to the 1st Battalion of 15th Artillery Division's 607th Cannon Artillery Regiment. The regiment was deployed in Ussuriysk and was "cropped," that is, only one battalion was combat-capable, while the remaining two battalions were supported by assigned personnel and deployed only in wartime. Lieutenant Colonel Mark Rafaelovich Ulanovsky was the commander of our battalion.

Our troop train – personnel in heated cars with pot-bellied stoves, and equipment on open platforms – moved to the scene of the combat operations, with a speed that was far from that of an express train. The stops, although not very long, were quite frequent. At each one there were many people, mostly women who were crying and who wanted us to persevere and stay alive. They gave us tasty food from their household supplies. I remember that our team got an enormous piece of the tastiest smoked bacon, which we ate for a long time at our fire position, recalling the kind words of that compassionate woman who gifted us with it as the train was pulling out. We couldn't help but recall the military newsreels of the 40s and seeing off our fathers to the front. History repeats itself. …

We arrived at the fire positions on 16 March 1969; they delivered ammunition all night. The next day, around lunchtime, we were busy with outfitting the positions; the command came: "Battery, to the battle!" And almost immediately: "For the infantry, 10 high-explosive fragmentation shells, quick fire!" There were six soldiers and two attached cadets in each gun team, that is, eight men served each cannon. We worked accurately and professionally.

We finished firing and remained for some time at the fire position; then we changed our position and no longer fired. All the combat work fit into one day. From our position we saw the flight of the rocket shells: this was the "Grads" at work.

I remember the arrival at our fire position of a large number of generals, headed by General of the Army I.G. Pavlovsky, commander-in-chief of the Ground Forces. We lined up and welcomed our distinguished guests. The Commander-in-Chief himself addressed the soldiers. He was friendly and good-natured toward the soldiers. He jokingly asked: "Why are you so grimy? Quickly clean yourselves up or else I'll give you the exercise narrative of 'The girls are coming!'" They stayed no more than 15 minutes at the fire position. After their departure and fatherly parting words, we cleaned ourselves up.

135th MRD scouts. (Military Museum of Hanoi, via Albert Grandolini)

Some of the enlisted men and sergeants who were veterans of the events refer to some mysterious lieutenant colonel who organised and supervised all intelligence activities during the Damansky events. For example, former sapper N.I. Nikiforov said that the Chinese used a loudspeaker to accuse the Soviets that 'Major [*sic*] Chernyi is stealing our people.' Another veteran, signalman V.M. Tirskikh, wrote the following about the man:

Some army intelligence department "came" to our line to replace artilleryman Borisenko. Lieutenant Colonel or Colonel Chernyi (I remember his deep base voice and felt that this man had great authority) with his equipment for detecting moving targets at night. Their reports: "I see four dots on the screen, in such-and-such an area of the island. ... moving in the direction of. ..."[3]

Judging by everything, he is talking about Lieutenant Colonel Yevgeny Yevstafyevich Chernyi, chief of intelligence of 135th MRD. Subordinated to him, in particular, was 131st Separate Reconnaissance Battalion. This battalion (Lieutenant Colonel G.P. Khrulev was the commander) appeared in the Damansky area on the night of 3 March, immediately after the first battle on the island. The main task of the scouts was to detect targets for subsequent destruction. The scouts were deployed at portable 'Podyem' radar stations, with a target-detection range of up to 10 kilometres.

From 3–6 March, scouts also searched for operating Chinese radio stations. One of the reports spoke about the first results of this work:

6 March 1969, the operation of a radio link at frequency 36150 was detected. The location of this link's radio station was determined by direction-finding posts.

- first radio station – in the Sanshenban area (4062);
- second radio station – dot 354.0 (3670);

The operation of a radio network at frequency 27890 kilohertz was established. Direction-finding posts determined the location of these radio stations:

- first radio station – in the Shumukhe area (3688);
- second radio station – in the Mount Shitoushan area (4402);
- third radio station – in the area of Hill 186.0, Nandatashan (3889);

The operation of the radio stations was intercepted with tape recordings.

Further on, right up to the 15 March battle, the scouts intercepted Chinese calls and searched nonstop for new radio stations.

Some lines from another report talk about the work of the separate intelligence battalion after 15 March:

An order was received on 15 March about assigning an intelligence group with the mission of searching throughout Damansky for wounded and dead, removing them from the island, capturing a prisoner, and collecting samples of shells, weapons, and other objects belonging to the Chinese soldiers.

The group operated in cooperation with the border guards. ...

At 4:50 the group began to move to Damansky Island. In front were members of the patrol: Junior Sergeant V.I. Krayushkin, Private G.V. Skramada, and Corporal Yu.A. Plotnikov. Surveillance established that there were no Chinese on the island.

Corporal B.G. Kanishchev was the first of the wounded to be discovered. The second was Private S.A. Maksimovich; this was quickly reported to Lieutenant A.M. Sizarev. The remaining personnel carried off the wounded from the island.

The group carefully examined 6 burned-up 60-P APCs; there were no wounded there; 2 burned corpses were discovered in the immediate vicinity of an APC, and 3 more dead soldiers were found next to them.

The scouts found a pile of every possible item. There were no Chinese on the island. It was namely this night on which the corpse of Colonel Leonov was found.

The scouts next went to Damansky on the night of 16–17 March. The goal of this raid was to cover the sappers who had mined the island, and to establish precisely where Leonov's tank was. The task was completely carried out. The scouts again gathered a pile of items, most of which were Chinese.

From these reports it becomes clearer how the 17 March events around Leonov's tank developed.

At around 17:30, the intelligence group, consisting of five men – Lieutenant M.G. Barkovsky, Junior Sergeant V.A. Bastrichkin, Private B.I. Loskutin, Private V.A. Proletsky, and Private P.I. Kochetkov – left for Damansky. After setting up a defence, the intelligence group signalled the recovery group.

As soon as the recovery group's vehicles appeared next to the damaged tank, Chinese artillery opened fire. In response, guns struck from the Soviet riverbank, suppressing the Chinese firing.

As is known, attempts to hook the tank were unsuccessful: one of the Soviet soldiers died and another was wounded. After this, the scouts received the task to evacuate. The intelligence group opened fire against the Chinese positions, and at this time the wounded and dead were tied with ropes and in this way were dragged to the tractor. Later, the scouts left the scene of the battle on this very tractor.

The events of 17 March are quite well known, so it is difficult to find any sensational evidence about this day.

Some authors, however, began to say that something happened on 17 March, which exceeded in scale the two well-known battles. For example, in the 15 December 1990 issue of the weekly, *Young Far Easterner*, an article entitled 'Mysterious Island. What Happened on Damansky in March 1969?' was published. The authors of the article, Yu. Pankov and A. Ryskin, cited, in particular, the recollections of Captain P.F. Vlasenko, the political officer of the artillery regiment's battalion:

On the sixteenth it seemed: there would be no repetition of anything. The next day I arrived at our battalion's observation post to relieve the battalion commander. "Comrade commander!" – in front of me was the on-duty soldier, with his eyes wide with horror. I ran to the instruments. … Oh! This had not happened before. As far as the eye could see along the horizon, a human mass was moving from the Chinese riverbank. In a band about two kilometres wide. Whereas before the fifteenth of March the Chinese had committed up to a regiment into battle, here … The first wave approached, pouring automatic bursts onto our riverbank. The second wave was moving about three hundred metres behind the first, and a third wave was farther off. The guns rolled and turned; they were preparing to fire … The battalion commander arrived and said: "Well, son, this is already war …" And the battle began. The Soviet people do not know about this day. The first volley was an ocean of defensive fire. There were only a few metres to Damansky – fire shifted to the Chinese riverbank.

Later in the article the authors themselves added the following:

The country was already enjoying peaceful everyday life: "The newspapers are silent – everything is calm!" For some reason, however, they were also silent about the fact that a real war had just begun.

It was like a crematorium. Several hundred Chinese soldiers died in the flames of the explosions of our rockets. A second attack came to replace the first, which had bogged down, and then a third came. In the two hours of artillery shelling, so much metal rained down on the heads of the attackers, that, according to estimates, it was as if each of our soldiers had shot 1½ –2 tons.

Recalling the Great Patriotic War, our artillerymen wrote on the shells that day: "Death to Mao!," "For the Motherland!" etc. Ground attack aircraft roared in the air. It didn't come to bombings, but they were ready.

In the evening, at half past seven, a command was sent to the battery: "Stop! Cease fire!" However, artillery was out of control: the political officers and commanders ran from gun to gun, forcibly pushing the soldiers away from the gun sights – the intoxication from the roaring, the smell of smoke, and the thrill of war was great.

When reading this excerpt, a number of questions naturally arise.

1. If the 17 March battle had reached such a scale, then why did veterans recall only the 2 and 15 March battles?

2. Before 15 March the Chinese had not known about the rocket artillery battalion. However, in the evening of that day, they learned from their own sad experience about the killing power of the 'Grads.' Why then did they drive their own soldiers to the slaughter?

3. Can anyone imagine a picture of how a Soviet soldier could, with one hand, push away an interfering political officer and with his other hand write on a shell 'Death to Mao!'?

It is true that, regarding the last question, the authors have a completely plausible theory. The fact is that one of the veterans of the conflict has a photograph of a group of Soviet soldiers loading a bomb into a mortar barrel. On the bomb an inscription written in white paint can be seen well – 'A gift to Mao.' The soldiers in the photo, however, look too carefree and ostentatious, and, therefore, even the least demanding researcher would be forced to admit that this is a hoax. The guys in this way simply decided to immortalise their involvement in the events, but the last thing we need is actors' information. It seems that the authors of this article used just such 'evidence' to write it.

None of the direct participants in the events confirm what was described above. It is also not certain that Political Officer Vlasenko did, in fact, say the words quoted above.

On the night of 17–18 March, a Soviet intelligence group went to Damansky once again. Now the command ordered that the presence of Chinese on the island be established and, in case they were discovered, a prisoner was to be taken. Chinese were detected, but nothing is certain about the capture of a prisoner.

The night of 18–19 March fell. Scouts went to Damansky and conducted a surveillance for Chinese.

The night of 19–20 March: an order came once again to cover the sappers and to look for Chinese on Damansky, and if the opportunity arose, to capture a prisoner. They found no Chinese. There was periodic machine-gun and automatic weapons fire along the island from the Chinese riverbank.

Meanwhile, on 20 March the servicemen from 199th Motorised Rifle Regiment who had died in the 15 March 1969 battle were buried in the village of Filino.

On the night of 20–21 March, the order for the scouts was that they determine approaches to the tank for the purpose of subsequently recovering it or blowing it up. Once again, a prisoner was needed.

The intelligence group came to the island and discovered a Chinese ambush near the damaged tank. The Chinese group was removing something from the T-62. Inasmuch as the number of Chinese was rather large, the scouts left after observing them.

On the night of 21–22 March, 135th Division's intelligence group was sent to damaged tank No. 545 in order to remove some instruments. At the same time, a Chinese intelligence group was located there. Sergeant Vasily Viktorovich Karmazin died in the ensuing crossfire. He was the last Soviet victim of the March clashes on the Ussuri River.

The 22 March 1969 issue of the Far Eastern Military District's newspaper, *Suvorovskiy natisk* [Suvorov Onslaught], described Karmazin and his comrades as follows:

A difficult combat task was assigned to a group of soldiers, headed by CPSU member Lieutenant M.G. Barkovsky, which would have to be carried out under strong fire from the Chinese riverbank. Furthermore, on its way to the target the group was ambushed by provocateurs. Communist Barkovsky, who had already carried out difficult tasks in battles near Damansky Island, exhibited composure, the ability to lead the battle, and personal bravery here. With his first volley he cut down one of the Maoists who had fired on our group, and wounded a second. The latter was still trying to shoot, but couldn't. The officer killed him with a light toss of a grenade.

With a precise massing of fire, Barkovsky's group was able to cover the soldiers headed by communist Shelest, who also decided the success of the operation.

However the Chinese provocateurs raged, raining mortar and machine-gun fire on the group of brave men and tossing grenades, they were unable to thwart the Soviet hero–soldiers. The difficult task assigned by the command was carried out.

In this intense fighting with the enemy, our soldiers Comrades Grigorenko and Sizarev distinguished themselves by their steadfastness and their fearlessness. Junior Sergeant V. Sanzharov, Sergeant V. Karmazin, and Sergeant V. Ryabtsev – Komsomol members who voluntarily requested to be part of this combat group – acted courageously. Wounded, they exhibited firmness of spirit and capably fought against the enemy. Glory to the brave defenders of the sacred borders of the Soviet Motherland![4]

The award citation for V.V. Karmazin reads as follows:

Supporting intelligence, the mining of the island, and the destruction of the tank, Sergeant V.V. Karmazin used his machine gun and grenades to cover the advance of the sapper group to the tank during the night battle, killing two Chinese who were waiting in ambush. In leading the fight, Sergeant V.V. Karmazin exhibited exceptional bravery, courage, and fearlessness. Changing position to assist the group's left flank, he was mortally wounded by a grenade explosion.[5]

In May, the personnel of the separate intelligence battalion returned to the place where they were permanently deployed.

The border guards also had a special group that was designated for sabotage operations. The following is what Tirskikh wrote about this:

A few words about the mysterious *spetsnaz*. A sabotage group, consisting of 15–20 men, was formed from detachment personnel. Kerichenko from the signal company, who worked on the telegraph key, was included in this group. I remember how we eagerly discussed their training to fire from all types of weapons and their night sorties to the island, and we enviously watched these guys. A short time later the group was disbanded.

Several independent and completely reliable sources are now saying that bystanders who were Soviet special services collaborators were on the Chinese riverbank during the Damansky events. Yu.V. Babansky recalls a man who was carrying out an intelligence mission:[6]

On one of the rainy nights we set off with our next mission – to meet with the Chinese agent. We had indicated a point on the map and named the meeting place. We arrived at the place. The agent wasn't there. We waited for a long time. A severe snowstorm was blowing, and I wondered if we had perhaps gone astray, if we had gotten lost. Or had the agent gotten lost? And where were we – on our own territory or on adjoining territory? Nothing was visible – it was nothing but snowy confusion!

Suddenly, automobile headlights pierced through the storm. Some kind of column was moving. I didn't know if it was ours or Chinese. I ordered the scouts to drop down, and I myself moved to meet the automobiles. It turned out the column was ours. That meant that we were on our own territory. And here, luckily our Chinese agent stepped out of the snowstorm. He was frozen, barely alive. He had also followed the headlight. We called the APC and brought the agent in it to the outpost.

We went to sleep, while the field officers busied themselves with the Chinese agent. They fed him, gave him something to drink, and gathered information. In the morning they woke our group up – we had to return the agent.

4

THERE WERE HEROES IN CHINA TOO

Each researcher of the conflict on Damansky Island at some moment probably discovered a strange symmetry: both sides fought with practically the same weapons, both wore headgear with red stars on the flaps, and in both the USSR and China the communists had summoned the soldiers to battle, etc.

This similarity can also be observed in the nature of the awards: among the Chinese participants in the battles on Damansky were also servicemen who received the 'Hero' medal, China's own version of the 'Hero of the Soviet Union' medal.

Here are the names of these men (in parentheses are cited the terms with which they were characterised in Chinese sources):

Yu Qingyang. (Chinese Internet)[1]

'Life does not stop, the attack does not stop.' Chinese propaganda poster dedicated to Yu Qingyang. (Chinese Internet)[2]

Yu Qingyang ('attack to the last breath'); Wang Qingrong ('eternal merit'); Chen Shaoguang ('a valiant death'); Yang Lin ('defender of the dignity of the Motherland'); Sun Zhengmin ('anti-mine hero'); Zhou Dengguo ('defence of the northern border'); Leng Pengfei ('the commander who is in front'); Hua Yujie ('valiant grenade launcher'); Du Yongchun ('energetic and valiant commander'); Sun Yuguo ('defence of the island').

The first five died in battle, the others survived. Materials that can be found on the Chinese Internet say why they all were honoured with the Hero medal. Naturally, not all information can be taken as truthful – much here has been painted in heroic colours; however, one can get some idea of the deeds of these men. Going down the list:

Yu Qingyang was born in September 1942 on the outskirts on the town of Pulandian in the province of Liaonin. He came from a peasant family. He entered military service in March 1963. In March 1969 he was in the reconnaissance platoon of 133rd Division's 397th Regiment. He received a serious head wound at the very beginning of the 2 March 1969 battle, and lost consciousness. After regaining consciousness he bandaged the wound by himself and rushed in to attack the enemy. At that moment a Soviet bullet cut him down on the spot. Dying, he allegedly said, 'Long live Chairman Mao. …'

It is difficult to say if all this actually happened, but there is even a propaganda poster in which soldier Yu is rushing into his last attack. Behind him is a medical orderly, whose face is frozen with fear – he seems to be saying where are you going in your condition? – and a couple of soldiers, one of whom is firing from a machine gun.

In 1998, a statue of Yu Qingyang was raised in the Memorial Park of Heroes in the town of Dalian (the administrative centre of Liaonin Province).

Wang Qingrong was born in 1940 in the county (*uezd*) of Santai, Sichuan Province. He came from a peasant family. He entered military service in 1959, and became a member of the CPC in 1961. In March 1969 he was a deputy company commander in 68th Division's 202nd Regiment. On the night of 1–2 March he set up an ambush with his soldiers on Damansky. He was seriously wounded in the chest and stomach in the battle at the moment when he

Wang Qingrong. (Chinese Internet)

Chen Shaoguang. (Chinese Internet)

Yang Lin. (Chinese Internet)

Sun Zhengmin. (Chinese Internet)

Zhou Dengguo. (Chinese Internet)

was trying to help another wounded soldier. In handing over the command, he said something like 'Hold, hold, fight for our land. ...' Dying, he held the head of a wounded soldier in one hand and fired at the enemy using a pistol with the other.

Chen Shaoguang was born in 1936 in the outskirts of the town of Ibin, Sichuan Province. He came from a peasant family. He entered military service in March 1959, and became a member of the CPC in 1961. In March 1969 he was deputy company commander in 133rd Division's 202nd Regiment. He was one of the model servicemen of Shenyang Military District, was awarded several medals, and was praised by the command. On the night of 2 March he was in an ambush on Damansky. In the 2 March battle he killed several of the enemy. He was wounded in the chest and right hand, and soon after died of his wounds. A high school in Ibin was named for him, and an obelisk was erected in his honour, and one of the bridges was named 'Bridge of the Hero' in his memory.

Yang Lin was born in September 1944 in the county of Dehui, Jilin Province. He came from a peasant family. He entered military service in August 1962, and had been a member of the CPC since 1968. In March 1969 he was an artilleryman, commander of a detachment in 3rd Battalion of 67th Division's 201st Regiment. In the 15 March battle he was in charge of a recoilless rifle team directly on Damansky. After the Soviet T-62 blew up on a mine, he took his weapon onto the ice and fired at the remaining three tanks, which resulted in one of them being put out of action. He then led a team of two guns and hit two enemy APCs. By this time, three of the fingers on Yang Lin's left hand had been crushed, and his right hand

was also damaged. He ordered the other soldiers to take cover, and then continued to fire from his gun, hitting another APC. As Yang Lin was aiming his gun, a shot from a Soviet tank ended his life.

Sun Zhengmin was born in 1936 in the county of Yessian, Shandong Province. He entered service with the PLA in 1951, and had been a member of the CPC since 1962. He graduated from a military-engineering academy. In March 1969 he was the commander of a sapper subunit. He was in charge of mine-laying on the ice of the Ussuri River, and it was namely one of these mines on which Leonov's tank blew up. In the 15 March battle he was involved with mine-clearing in order to create passages for reinforcements. In the days that followed he also cleared the island of mines. He died on 20 March 1969 when a mine exploded (in a different version, he was killed by a Soviet sniper).

Zhou Dengguo was born in September 1943 in the town of Pengshui, Sichuan Province. He entered the army in September

Leng Pengfei reads a newspaper to his subordinates. (Military Museum of Hanoi, via Albert Grandolini)

Hua Yujie. (Chinese Internet)

1943, and was a member of the CPC since 1965. In March 1969 he was a detachment commander in 133rd Division's 398th Regiment. It was namely he who fired the first shot, killing Strelnikov. He was wounded and was sent to a hospital. He took part in the 15 March battle, killing two of the enemy.

Leng Pengfei was born in January 1933 in the county of Xishui, Hubei Province. He was a member of the CPC since 1954. He entered military service in 1956. He was awarded many medals and was praised by the command for his good service. In March 1969 he was commander of 1st Battalion of 68th Division's 202nd Regiment. In the 15 March battle he commanded the repelling of the first and second attack by the Soviet APCs with infantry, and was in charge of the antitank grenade-launcher fire. As a result, the enemy suffered substantial casualties, including two damaged APCs. He was wounded in the left hand, but continued to guide the battle until he was brought off the battlefield.

Hua Yujie was born in 1945 in the county of Bosian, Anhui Province. He entered the PLA in 1965, and has been a member of the CPC since 1969. In March 1969 he was a grenade launcher in 68th Division's 202nd Regiment. At the beginning of the 15 March battle, he took two APCs out of action with a handheld antitank grenade launcher. When enemy soldiers jumped out of the damaged APCs,

Du Yongchun. (Chinese Internet)

Sun Yuguo (on the right). (Chinese Internet)

he fired at them with a machine gun. He almost went deaf from the roar of the shots from his grenade launcher, but he continued to fight. On that day he took a total of four APCs out of action.

Du Yongchun was born in 1943 in the town of Harbin. He entered army service in 1962, and has been a member of the CPC since 1965. He was a political worker in 133rd Division. In the 2 March 1969 battle he killed two enemy soldiers with a grenade. In the 15 March battle he was in charge of a group of 11 soldiers, who defended their position on the island for 9 hours. During breaks he organised meetings, summarising his battle experience.

Sun Yuguo was born in 1944 in the town of Shenyang. He joined the PLA in 1961, and has been a member of the CPC since 1964. In December 1967 he became the chief of the Hunsy Chinese border post. He took part in 22 border skirmishes. On 2 March he brought 30 soldiers to the ice of the Ussuri River and led the heavy firing against Strelnikov's group.

As the text from one of the propaganda posters states, Sun Yuguo and his subordinates killed all the enemies in 17 minutes. Does this mean that for this amount of time they exchanged fire with Rabovich's group of border guards, or that for 17 minutes the Chinese were looking for the dead from Strelnikov's group and they collected equipment? No one knows.

It is said that Sun Yuguo also took part in the 15 March battle.

Sun Yuguo was sent to the IX Congress of the CPC, where he was given the platform for an address. Chinese documentary film footage reported to viewers the mood of the hall at that moment: here Sun Yuguo is rushing to Mao to shake his hand; everyone stands. … Sun is too agitated to stand in place, he waves his hands and shouts something to the audience. Having shaken Mao Zedong's hand, Sun moves in the direction of Zhou Enlai, but Mao pulls him in another direction, toward Lin Biao; after all, Marshal Lin occupies the second position in the leadership. Sun shakes Lin Biao's hand, and only now reaches over to Zhou Enlai. Premier Zhou joyfully says something, and behind him an excited Jiang Qing appears. … The last footage of this episode is inadvertently sober: Mao is sitting in his place and with a mockingly ominous grin on his face, as if silently assessing everything that is taking place.

Now we have the opportunity to find out how official PRC propaganda presented the events of March 1969 to the Chinese people. The attentive reader hardly requires special explanations: already knowing the actual course of events, one can easily distinguish the truth from lies and inaccuracies from deliberate falsification.

In 1992, Chinese authors Chen Zhibing and Sun Xiao wrote an article about the events on Damansky.[3] The following is a considerably abridged version of what they wrote about the 2 March battle:

At night a reconnaissance detachment came to the island. In addition to weapons, they had taken biscuits and 100 grams of vodka per man.

The temperature was less than -30° C. The scouts piled up snow and kept each other from falling asleep.

At around 6:00 in the morning on 2 March, a jeep approached from the direction of the USSR toward the southern tip of Zhenbao. Two men got out of the jeep, one of them was Lieutenant Colonel Yanshin. Some time later they left.

Sun and Zhou[4] arrived at the island with their groups, Sun in front and Zhou behind him. Two APCs, a military truck, and the command vehicle arrived from the two Soviet outposts. Soviet soldiers left for the eastern part of the island and blocked the Chinese patrol.

All 70 Soviet soldiers had machine guns, but there were no mountings. Sun said to his men that they should be on their guard and be ready to fight back. One group of Soviet soldiers began to move to the left, and the other group to the right, in order to encircle the Chinese soldiers. Sun then ordered a withdrawal to the west.

Sun knew that the Soviet soldiers might shoot, and, therefore, he loudly cried out: "Defend the nation!" As soon as the Chinese border guards fanned out, the Soviet soldiers began to fire. Sun warned the Soviets, but the Soviet soldiers disregarded the warning and continued to fire. Ma[5] then ordered the Chinese to fight back.

One Soviet APC approached from the east and started to circle the island. The Chinese soldiers used rockets, but they did not hit their targets because the shooters were novices. The APC went back.

The Chinese counterattacked, killing several Soviet soldiers.

Chen Shaoguang was hit by a bullet, and he began to bandage it. Although Chen was wounded, he continued to command. Yu Qingyang died.

Ma said that we had to withdraw, because Chen was wounded and Deputy Company Commander Wang was dead. The Chinese began to withdraw. Shi Rongting took a camera and Sun Baosan and Zhou Xijin took five machine guns.

Ivan spotted the Chinese withdrawal and began to pursue.… Shooting could be heard from the centre of the Island, and the Chinese understood that the Soviet soldiers had begun to fire, because they heard Zhou Dengguo's voice.

Ivan intended to open fire, but he himself was killed by Zhou Dengguo, who had outrun him. All 7 Soviet soldiers who had been with him were also killed.

The Chinese patrol withdrew from the forest to the edge of Zhenbao; the Soviet soldiers continued firing in the distance. Some Chinese soldiers carried Chen Shaoguang on a stretcher, others made a list of the dead. Everyone was gloomy and silent. A little later a military doctor arrived. He injected Chen Shaoguang with a stimulant. Chen slowly opened his eyes and said: "I am dying. Don't curse the doctor." Many started to cry.

Commander Ma angrily said: "Don't cry. Crying won't revive him." But after this he himself started to cry.

On 2 March 1969, a Soviet patrol provoked this conflict, as a result of which relations between China and the USSR became even worse. Two border patrols did, in fact, fight one another.

Later on the authors describe the 15 March 1969 battle:

On 15 March at 3:00 AM, Yu Hongdong heard a strange sound and threw a rock to signal. A little later 6 APCs with soldiers showed up. More than 30 soldiers with machine guns dismounted and slowly set off for the island.

Having observed all this, Yu said: "The enemy is 30 meters away. Should I open fire?"

Xiao Quanfu answered: "I assume that they have not seen us. In any case, we cannot be the first to open fire. Otherwise, we will make a major political error."

Then he continued: "They will want to kill us after we leave for the island in the morning. But we will be first. Tell Yu Hongdong that he should hide carefully. Artillery should block the river so

that Soviet tanks cannot cross it. Soldiers of 23rd Army should use grenade launchers against the APCs. …"

At 8:00 in the morning the Chinese patrol began to circle the island. Sun Yuguo was in charge of a group of 12 men. They moved from south to north. When they had reached the middle of the island, they stopped, because Sun Yuguo knew of the presence of Soviet soldiers in the forest. After he detected the movement of the enemy to the riverbank, he ordered the group to return.

The Soviets observed the withdrawal of the Chinese patrol and prepared to be the first to open fire in order to not allow the Chinese soldiers to leave. As soon as the Soviet soldiers were the first to open fire, Sun Yuguo ordered his men to take cover. Commander Leonov saw this through his binoculars and ordered his second-line troops to fire. At 8:05, 3 Soviet APCs and 20 infantrymen attacked the Chinese patrol. They were in front of Yu Hongdong. Yu said: "Prepare to fire."

The Chinese soldiers aimed at the enemy. "Fifty meters, forty, thirty. …" Finally Yu ordered: "Fire!"

All types of weapons opened fire. The Soviet soldiers were forced to withdraw. An hour later the first Soviet attack ended in failure. The Soviets lost more than ten men and one APC. …

Leonov was not upset about the failure of the first attack. He had not known about the Chinese soldiers hidden on the island, but now he had discovered them. Once again he gathered a detachment of 3 tanks and 3 APCs. Lieutenant Colonel Yanshin was in charge of four tanks to cut off communication with the island and kill the Chinese. On 15 March at 9:46, the second attack commenced. The Soviets had very powerful artillery. Yu Hongdong ordered that rounds be conserved and that the soldiers fire only at close range.

Yu Hongdong was in charge of fire from the grenade launchers and guns; as a result, one APC was knocked out of action. The Soviet infantry went to ground and moved neither forward nor back. Soviet tanks also stopped on the river's ice, but continued to fire. The other 4 tanks began to encircle the Chinese, moving around the southern tip of the island. Yu Hongdong was thrilled: now the antitank mines would go to work! He ordered soldier Zhou Xijin to fire on the Soviet tanks with the grenade launcher. …

If the antitank mines had not worked, this would have had serious consequences. The attack renewed from the eastern part of the island, and our soldiers suffered casualties.

Commander 4th Class Shi Rongting killed many of the enemy, so that the Soviets did not dare show themselves again.

Du Yongchun's detachment also acted bravely and destroyed one APC that was transporting soldiers. A little later one of the tanks blew up on mines. …

Two hours later, the Soviet attack failed once again. At 15:13 the Soviets again opened fire. 15 minutes later, 24 tanks and APCs and an infantry company began a powerful attack. Leng Pengfei, a commander from 77th Division, was in charge of reinforcement and set off for the island.

Du Yongchun recognised the enemy commander and loudly said that they should fire at the man dressed in a black fur coat. Leonov was to command more than 70 tanks in the attack across the river. Suddenly, one of the shells hit the command post and demolished it. At that moment Leonov had stood up, and a bullet struck him directly in the heart.

A curious fact: Ma Xianjie, an 'intelligence specialist in 133rd Division' who was in charge of the Chinese ambush on 2 March, was not honoured with the Hero medal. Judging by everything, the results of the first battle were not what the Chinese commanders had counted on.

It should be mentioned that as long as the issue was about heroes from a formal point of view, that is, about those Chinese servicemen who were awarded this title, they received the corresponding medal and certifying documents. However, in Chinese literature and the mass media, it was accepted to call all those who died in battle heroes and martyrs. And so how many there were of them and what their names were is a major question. Estimating the Chinese casualties immediately after the end of the 15 March battle, Soviet border guards gave a figure of 600–800 dead alone. Radio-interception specialists and artillery observers came up with approximately the same figures. Those who saw the 'Grad' volleys describe in practically the same way a sharp change in the situation in the area of the island: before the strike – intensive firing and a shift of a large number of infantry on the Chinese riverbank; after the strike – thick smoke and the absence of any signs of life on the Chinese side. It was even clear from the outside how heavy the Chinese casualties were. A year later, however, the cited figures had to be corrected, and it was an incredible event that contributed to this.

In summer 1970, a Chinese commander crossed the Ussuri River. He acted daringly: taking his machine gun with him, in broad daylight he jumped into the water and swam for dear life to the Soviet riverbank.

When questioned, the defector said he was a platoon leader. He explained his action as being a disagreement with the policies of Mao Zedong, as well as being a personal motive – his father, mother, and wife had all died of starvation. With regard to the latter circumstance, the defector added that the command had offended him by not allowing him to attend the funeral of his relatives.

It is significant that, despite all the Maoist propaganda, which depicted Soviet activities in the blackest of colours, the Chinese commander had defected to just these 'Soviet revisionists.'

Among other things, he was asked about Chinese casualties during the conflict of the previous year. He answered that all who had died on Damansky Island had been buried in three large mounds, not far from the scene of the conflict. The defector himself had been at the burial, and although he did not know the precise number of those who had been buried there, older comrades had said that *several hundred* bodies had been placed in each grave. Thus, if the word *several* is treated as 2, even as a minimum, the one gets the figure of 600. Most probably there were significantly more dead, because, if 200 people were buried in a mound, then they would say '200.' Yet here he said 'several hundred.'

Since that time, there has been no new information about the number of dead Chinese; therefore, the numbers 200, 600, 800, etc. that we catch sight of in domestic and foreign publications cannot be considered reliable.[6] One can only remark that the number 800 is most often mentioned but, that being said, the authors of those publications cannot articulately explain how they came up with this number. Moreover, these authors are beginning to cite one another, creating a vicious circle.

Much could be cleared up if that defector came forward (if, indeed, he is still alive). Generally in the USSR, there was the practice of sending all defectors to special settlements. These settlements were located in Siberia and existed literally until the *perestroika* era. Many defectors had started families there and then began to disperse throughout all of Russia. They did not return to China, inasmuch as there they are still considered to be traitors. Even during Mao's regime the Soviet authorities tried to send the PRC citizens who had fled back to their motherland, but they immediately rejected this practice because the trial and punishment for the 'traitors' were done at the borderline.

Obviously, it would not have been difficult to find the defector if the workers of the appropriate organs had troubled themselves with this problem. Unfortunately, in this matter, their help is not expected.

It seems that the number of dead PLA soldiers and commanders is the main secret that the Chinese are carefully protecting. For the sake of keeping this secret, a memorial cemetery was created in the small county town of Baoqing, where the Chinese servicemen killed on Damansky are buried. A little was said about this cemetery in a previous chapter, when Chinese casualties in the 2 March battle were discussed. Let us now discuss it in a little more detail.[7]

The memorial complex is enclosed on all sides with a brick fence. When entering, the memorial director's office, additional buildings, and a shop are located on the right and left. Walking directly along an alley, visitors at first pass through the Hall of Glory, and then come to rest in the main building – the memorial to those who died on Damansky. The memorial is made of a light stone and is a genre scene – a group of servicemen are fighting for the island. The central scene is that of the commander, with his right arm raised, in which a pistol is clutched, with the barrel upright. It is evident that a shot from this pistol is to call the soldiers to attack. The officer's mouth is open – not only is he firing into the air, but also his shout is inspiring his subordinates. In front of the commander are two PLA privates: one, in a seated position, is aiming an RPG-2 grenade launcher; the other is moving forward with a machine gun at the ready. To the left, another soldier is setting up something resembling a mortar, and yet another soldier, behind him, is waving a grenade. On the lateral surfaces, the base of the monument are panels depicting different episodes of the battle.

Immediately behind the memorial, those five servicemen who were awarded the Hero of the PLA medal are buried. The gravestones are made of red marble, on each of which is a photograph of the dead soldier and a brief biography.

The burial sites of the other 63 PLA soldiers are located immediately behind the graves of the 'heroes.' They look somewhat more meagre – they are made of grey granite – but they also have photos and red stars on the gravestones.

To the left of the memorial to those who died on Zhenbao is another monument – to those who fell during the liberation of Baoqing in 1945. Their names are carved out on four vertical gravestones.

Entrance to the memorial area is free only for PRC citizens. As for foreigners (especially Russians), they are allowed into the area only with written permission from the local authorities.

Here are the names of those who died on Damansky (and the dates of their death) from 14-26 March 1969, which are carved on the gravestones: 14 March: Wang Zhiyou, Lü Wenhui; 15 March: Yang Lin, Xi Hongda, Yuan Qifa, Zhu Chaoyu, Li Shanglie, Xiang Yili, Chen Yongcai, Zhang Zhengwan, Yao Pilu, Zhen Daoxun, Li Fengxiang, Wu Wenjun; 17 March: An Baofeng, Zhao Shitou; 18 March: Tan Zuwan, Tang Zhengzhi; 20 March: Sun Zhengmin; 24 March: Zhang Yinhua, Chen Zhongjun, Dong Shuhuan; 26 March: Gao Weihan

After the battle on Damansky ended, the Soviets set up a fire cover of the island, right up until the negotiations between A.N. Kosygin and Zhou Enlai on 11 September 1969. During this time nine PLA servicemen died: Chen Zunru (7 April), Dong Mingchun (12 April), Zhang Rongkuan (15 April), Fu Renyuan (21 April), Li Xicai (7 June), Liu Jidie (16 June), Li Yongfa (16 June), Liu Tingshou (16 August), Chen Qiying (5 September).

Finally, there is a list of those who died quite some time after the end of combat operations: Li Fuchun (26 November), Zou Yongqing (30 November), Zhang Shuquan (30 May 1970), Li Zhenging (3 July 1970), Song Heyuan (4 July 1970), Lin Dongfa (19 September 1970), Lu Zhongwen (2 April 1971), Gao Minyuan (7 June 1971), Huang Wencheng (7 June 1971), Liang Zhanqi (7 June 1971), Chen Guohua (21 June 1971), Ren Dongsheng (27 April 1972), Liu Kechuang (21 June 1972), Zhang Guoqing (25 May, year is illegible), Song Yinkang (23 September, year is illegible).

Returning to the theme of the number of Chinese who died on 15 March 1969, it is natural to ask: how can we understand the improbably low number of dead – 12 men? Most probably it is another burial ground that the defector was talking about. Tourists

are probably not taken there, inasmuch as it would be necessary otherwise to talk about heavy casualties, and the Chinese do not need that kind of truth today.

In general, the fact that different Chinese sources cite different figures for their own casualties – one says 32, another one says 68, still another says 71, etc. – calls attention to itself. Evidently, there has been a clear attempt to not get into a fix: to cite figures that are too high would mean to be called on the carpet by the chief for deviating from the party line; to cite figures that are too low – no one would believe them.

In any case, the General Staff of the PLA knows the precise answer to this question (or could find out if it wants to).

5
FROM DULATY TO KIRKINSKY

The events on Damansky Island produced a stunning impression on Soviet and Chinese citizens. They and others could not ultimately believe that yesterday's allies, comrades, and brothers were fighting in a fierce battle for a small border island. Other conflicts on the Sino-Soviet border were somehow lost in the shadow of Damansky, and although they were not on the same scale, they still were accompanied by both military and civilian casualties.

On the morning of 2 May 1969, a group of Chinese shepherds crossed the USSR border at the sector patrolled by the 3rd Border Outpost (Dulaty) of the Eastern Border District's Bakhtinsky Border Detachment (Kazakh SSR). The shepherds were driving a flock of sheep along a special path, which they had been given permission

to use, in accordance with an agreement with Soviet authorities. On this day, however, the rules of the use of Soviet territory were violated.[1]

Passage along the path envisioned coordination with the Soviet border guards, as well as continuous observation on their part. The Chinese had been strictly observing this arrangement, but on 2 May they crossed the border without having given any notification. In addition, whereas usually 3–5 shepherds drove the flocks, this time there were 30 of them.

The border detail reported to the outpost what was happening. Some time later, a group of border guards (a total of 16 men), headed by Major Zagidullin, arrived at the scene of the events.

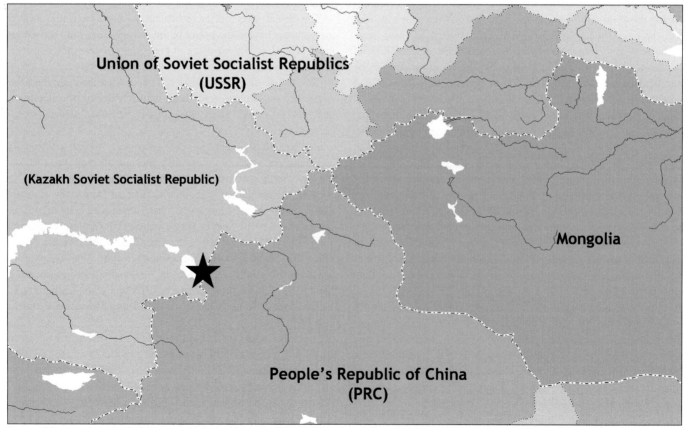

Scene of the events in the Dulaty area is indicated by a star. (Map by Tom Cooper based on authors' inscriptions on original contour map)

The border guards stopped the shepherds, but attempts to drive them out were unsuccessful. Suddenly, around 50 Chinese servicemen appeared, shouting threats at the border guards, and then a few more groups of Chinese, with up to 30 men in each, crossed the border. One of the Chinese shouted: 'We are on our own territory! This is not the same thing as Damansky Island!' Then, two cameramen filmed continuously. Inasmuch as the numerical superiority of the Chinese was considerable, Major Zagidullin ordered his subordinates to withdraw.

Chinese soldiers began to occupy convenient positions on the hills and entrench themselves. The depth of the penetration into Soviet territory was three kilometres, and eight kilometres along the front. It became clear that the Chinese were conducting some kind of confrontational operation. A report that not only PRC border guards, but also regular army soldiers were taking part in the incident at the border was very alarming.

Lieutenant Colonel A.Ya. Panshentsev, chief of the Bakhtinsky Border Detachment, reported what was happening to General Lieutenant M.K. Merkulov, chief of the Border District. A decision was made to try to resolve the problem that had arisen by negotiations, but at the same time to prepare a full-fledged operation to drive the Chinese from Soviet territory.

Manoeuvre groups from the Bakhtinsky and neighbouring Uch-Aral Border Detachments were sent to the scene of the events, and the neighbouring Tasty and Uzun-Bulak Outposts raised the alarm. A total of around 600 men and more than three dozen APCs were involved. An officer meeting developed a plan for further operations, the line of demarcation, and arrangements for communications.

During the first day, the border guards were busy outfitting the territory – they dug trenches and caponiers for the APCs, and prepared positions for machine guns and grenade launchers. Terrain conditions were such, that camouflage was practically impossible: there were only hills with sparse brush all around.

An operations group, headed by Colonel B.I. Kolodyazhnyi, chief of staff of the border district (he was replaced on 10 May by General Major B.M. Golubev, deputy chief of the district), was formed to direct the assembled subunits. The initial operations plan envisioned the border guards conducting an operation to drive out the Chinese by force. The make-up of the assault group and the initial lines for the attack were determined quite quickly, and tasks were assigned to the auxiliary services.

The Chinese were also actively preparing for combat operations: PLA units were brought up from the depth of Chinese territory, and artillery appeared. By 5 May, two Chinese Army battalions were located directly on Soviet territory.

Veteran V.I. Gladkov recalls the following:

An excellent combat attitude ruled in the subunits; there was not a single case of weakness or panic. We, the officers, had been provided with very good personnel at that time. We all, as one, exhibited patriotism – not literary, but real patriotism. The political officers did not have to have special talks with us – the soldiers remembered the example of Damansky and were ready to fight.

The time approached for the commencement of the operation; however, no order had been received. It turned out that the forces of the "neighbours" had increased so much over the past day, that the command was not going to send the border guards against the enemy's clearly superior forces. Only a note from the USSR M[inistry] of F[oreign] A[ffairs] was sent, with the demand that the Chinese leave Soviet territory.[2]

The build-up of regular Chinese troops forced the Soviet command to engage units from the Turkestan Military District (General of the Army N.G. Lyashenko – commander).

Motorised rifle, tank, and artillery subunits and two 'Grad' battalions were sent to the scene of the events. If it had been necessary, an airfield had been prepared for air support in the Uch-Aral District, at which a fighter bomber regiment was located. The deployment had been done openly and pointedly, for the purpose of sobering up the opposing side and keeping the Chinese commanders from doing anything foolhardy.

With regard to the fact that the principal role in conducting a full-fledged operation was handed over to the army, the tasks of the border guards changed. Their principal duty was to conduct surveillance and reconnaissance, and to cover the flanks of the grouping that had been formed.

I.I. Petrov (deputy chief of the political department of the Eastern Border District at the time of the events) recalled the following:

On the night of 3 May, a group of provocateurs, under cover of night, attempted to reach the area of our deployment. A heavy rain and fog made surveillance of them difficult. All details had been warned about the need for high vigilance, and the soldiers handled their tasks well. When the group of provocateurs attempted to reconnoitre our positions in the sector where Corporal Pavel Kryachko was patrolling, they were immediately discovered, after which they successfully left.[3]

In turn, the Soviets several times organised reconnaissance operations on the hills occupied by the Chinese. Thus, on the night of 5 May, Lieutenant D. Shamritsky and Lieutenant V. Korolev were in charge of a group of 20 men, who had arrived at the crest of one of the hills. Having caught sight of the border guards, the Chinese immediately hid in their shelter, while the Soviet scouts carefully studied the enemy's positions. The actions of other groups of border guards on the night of 8–9 May were just as successful.

For the two weeks of confrontation on the border, the Soviets conducted intense counterpropaganda. For this they used a powerful broadcasting station set up in the centre of the combat formations, and two lightweight border broadcasting stations located on the flanks. Twice a day, the announcement from the USSR Government, dated 29 March 1969, and the texts of two Soviet newspaper articles that had gained fame – 'What History Teaches' and 'The Depth of Betrayal' – were broadcast in Chinese.

The Chinese also made broadcasts, using notes from Peking radio programs. As a rule, these broadcasts presented the Chinese version of events on Damansky Island, sent out challenges to reject revisionism, and presented territorial claims to the Soviet Union. The lightweight Soviet broadcasting stations jammed the Chinese transmissions with concert programs for the border guards.

Natural conditions in the area of the events did very little to contribute to a comfortable deployment for the troops. Nevertheless, appropriate services were provided: personnel received three hot meals, and were provided newspapers, letters, packages, and tobacco products. Community showers were organised in field bathhouses, a change of underwear was provided, and movies were regularly shown.

The Dulaty events ended as unexpectedly as they had begun. Apparently, two circumstances influenced the Chinese – the efforts of Soviet diplomats with regard to a peaceful resolution of the situation that had arisen, and the demonstration of overwhelming military force, organised by the Turkestan Military District command and

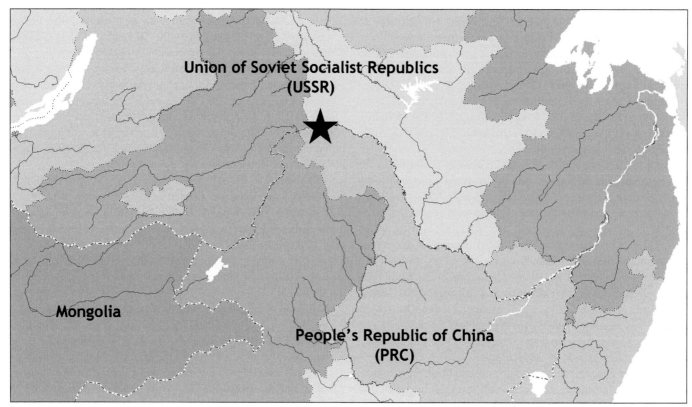

The location of Kultuk Island is indicated by a star on the map of the Far East. (Map by Tom Cooper based on authors' inscriptions on original contour map)

the command of border guards. Beginning on 15 May, the number of border violations began to decrease, and by 18 May the Chinese has completely left Soviet territory. A few days later, the Turkestan Border District began to withdraw its subunits.

The border guards had set up tent camps between the Tasty and Dulaty Outposts. Reinforced details, headed by officers, did their service there. As subsequent events showed, these preventative measures were a good idea.

In May 1969, another conflict took place – this time in the area of Kultuk Island.

Kultuk Island is located on the Amur River (53° 20' 55" northern latitude, 124° 7' 31" eastern longitude). In 1969 it was a part of the Magadachinsky District of the Amur *Oblast*, and was in the area of responsibility of the Far Eastern Military District's 55th Dzhalindinsky Border Detachment. The length of the island was approximately 1,400 metres, and its maximum width was on the order of 270 metres. The nearest populated area was the village of Albazino.

The villagers visited the island from time to time, for the purpose of haymaking. In 1969, the Chinese also started to come to Kultuk. At first the Soviet border guards did not react to this at all; however, when a wooden house appeared on the island, it became clear that the 'neighbours' were trying to gain a foothold on Soviet territory. The protests and warnings addressed to the Chinese had no effect. During the first days of May, activities of Chinese soldiers were noticed on the sector opposite the island.

On one night, a group of Chinese broke into the house on the island and hid there. All this looked as if an ambush had been set up there.

Using a loudspeaker, the border guards demanded that the Chinese leave Soviet territory. They warned them that force would be used if they did not comply with this demand. Inasmuch as there was no reaction to this, a decision was made to fire incendiary

bullets at the house. As soon as the house caught fire, the Chinese left their shelter and withdrew to their own territory.

Because further actions from the neighbouring side were difficult to forecast, an operations headquarters was set up at the scene of the events, headed by General A.F. Onishenko, first deputy chief of troops of the Far Eastern Border District. Bearing in mind the surprise Chinese attack on Damansky, it was decided not to go to the island, but rather to cover it with fire.

Trenches were dug on the Soviet bank of the Amur and positions were equipped in case of a Chinese invasion; communications were set up, and timely hot food was organised. The border guards received heavy machine guns and night-vision instruments.

From a tactical point of view, the Chinese positions were more favourable in two respects. Firstly, the dominating heights were on their side of the river. Secondly, the river bent in this area, and, therefore, the adjacent territory enveloped Kultuk in a semi-circle. In case a battle erupted, the island would have been in a semi-circle of enemy fire resources. However, the matter did not come to an armed clash.

By mid-May, tensions had begun to lessen, and gradually disappeared. Most probably, the Chinese command came to the conclusion that the Soviets were ready to repel them fiercely, and that they had lost any possibility of surprise.

The Soviet press did not report a single word about the events on Kultuk Island.

Nevertheless, after the events at Dulaty, the situation on the western sector of the Sino-Soviet border near Dulaty had still not stabilised. Once again the Chinese instigated a dangerous conflict in this very area, using the already tested method of herding livestock across Soviet territory.

On 11 June 1969, the USSR MFA sent the following note to the PRC MFA:

Chinese drive livestock through Soviet territory. (Chinese Internet)

the Chinese authorities at the above-mentioned border sector, the Chinese not only have not made the necessary conclusions, but also, as the actions of 10 June of this year attest, have set off on a path that further complicates the situation on this border sector.

The USSR Ministry of Foreign Affairs is lodging a decisive protest with the PRC Ministry of Foreign Affairs because of this new scheme of the Chinese authorities, and demands that decisive measures be taken to put an end to the escalation of tensions on the sector of the Sino-Soviet border in the area of the Tasty River.

Responsibility for the serious consequences of provocative actions by the Chinese authorities wholly lie with the Chinese.

Moscow, 11 June 1969.[4]

The events that were briefly discussed in the note unfolded this way.

On 10 June, a border detail that was located near the Burgon secret surveillance post noticed on the adjacent side a flock of sheep, numbering around 100 heads, which a Chinese shepherd was herding. Having violated the rules of crossing the state border, the shepherd went into Soviet territory. A group of 10 Soviet border guards, under the command of Lieutenant I.S. Litvinov, advanced to meet him. Using a Russian–Chinese phrasebook, the officer demanded that he leave Soviet territory. However, the politically-savvy shepherd took out a book of Mao's quotations, and in response began to spew forth slogans (Chinese sources say that his name was Zhang Chengshan).

An alarm group, headed by Sergeant N. Krasikov from the Tasty Outpost, arrived on horseback, after which the border guards went to arrest the shepherd. Twelve Chinese soldiers appeared from out of their shelter, headed by an officer with his weapon ready.

At some moment Sergeant V. Mashinets, one of the border guards, heard the distinctive sound of machine gun bolts being pulled back, and he shouted: 'Drop!' The border guards instantly followed his command and the Chinese immediately began to shoot. An exchange of fire ensured.

The Chinese tried to bring reinforcements – around 20 soldiers on horseback – into the battle, but this group was stopped by the machine gun team of Private V. Shchugarev and Private M. Boldyrev.

During the fighting Sergeant Krasikov was seriously wounded and was brought to the outpost on horseback. Unfortunately, he could not be saved.

About 20 minutes after the battle began, a motorised manoeuvre group on APCs rushed to the scene of the events. Deploying in combat formation, the border guards prepared to repel a possible Chinese invasion. Some time later, a helicopter arrived here,

Note from the USSR Ministry of Foreign Affairs to the PRC MFA
The Ministry of Foreign Affairs of the Union of Soviet Socialist Republics declares the following to the Ministry of Foreign Affairs of the People's Republic of China.

The PRC MFA published a note which crudely distorted the events that took place on 10 June of this year on the Sino-Soviet border in the area of the Tasty River (Semipalatinsk *Oblast*)

In fact, the event transpired in the following way.

On 10 June 1969, the Chinese authorities organised a new provocation on the Sino-Soviet border in this region.

To cover up this latest scheme, the Chinese authorities, as before, used herdsmen with a flock of sheep.

On 10 June at 18:00, a Chinese citizen with a flock of sheep crossed the Soviet border into the above-mentioned area and went 400 metres into Soviet territory. A group of Chinese servicemen, who had covertly invaded the territory of the USSR, supported the border violation.

In response to the demands of the Soviet border guards to the border violators that they must leave Soviet territory, the Chinese servicemen suddenly opened fire from machine guns against the Soviet border detail. The Soviet border detail, in self-defence, was forced to open retaliatory fire, after which the violators left the territory of the USSR.

As for the statements contained in the Chinese note about the Soviets' alleged employment of tanks and armoured personnel carriers, all this is an idle fabrication to pursue belligerent goals.

Despite the strict warning made by the USSR Ministry of Foreign Affairs to the PRC Ministry of Foreign Affairs in the note dated 4 May of this year concerning the defiant actions of

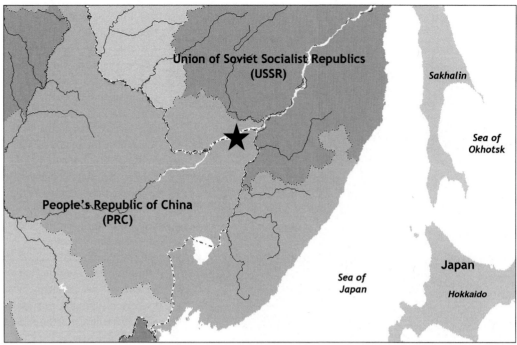

Location of Goldinsky Island on the map indicated by the star. (Map by Tom Cooper based on authors' inscriptions on original contour map)

On 8 July 1969, a group of Soviet rivermen (nine men in all) left for the Soviet side of Goldinsky for maintenance on nautical signs, as it had been accepted before. The Chinese, who had secretly made their way to the island and set up an ambush, suddenly opened fire from machine guns and then used grenades. As a result, one riverman (Aleksei Khandoga, 22 years old) died and three Soviet citizens were wounded. The boats *Turpan* and *Drozd*, on which the rivermen had come, were damaged.

Upon the appearance of Soviet border guards, the Chinese ran to their side of the island, having left behind property belonging to them, including notes with plans for the provocation. They learned from these notes that the attack on the riverman had been planned in advance, and the purpose of the attack was to kill Soviet citizens.

The Chinese provocation looked especially brazen, inasmuch as at this very time the Sino-Soviet commission on shipping on the border rivers was being held in Khabarovsk.

On 8 July 1969, the PRC embassy in Moscow was handed the following note regarding the events on Goldinsky Island:

Note from the USSR Minister of Foreign Affairs to the PRC embassy in Moscow

The Ministry of Foreign Affairs of the Union of Soviet Socialist Republics declares the following to the embassy of the People's Republic of China.

On 8 July of this year at 10 hours and 30 minutes, a group of armed Chinese, having violated the state border of the USSR and hidden themselves on the Soviet part of Goldinsky Island on the Amur River, opened fire from machine guns against Soviet rivermen–track workers, who had come to this island for repair work on navigation signs, as had often been done before. The attackers also used grenade launchers and hand grenades.

As a result of this predatory attack on the unarmed Soviet rivermen, who were carrying out their official responsibilities, one of them was killed and three were wounded. The riverboats "Drozd" and "Turpan" were seriously damaged.

The Soviet rivermen–track workers on Goldinsky Island were acting in strict accordance with the Sino-Soviet agreement of 1951 concerning the policy for sailing on the Amur, Ussuri, Argun, and Sungacha border rivers and Khanka Island, and concerning the establishment of shipping on these waterways. The Chinese know that navigation signs had been set up on this island, and that the Soviets have always maintained them and continue to do so.

The above-mentioned armed bandit attack on the Soviet rivermen on 8 July of this year is a vile provocation, aimed at exacerbating the situation on the border sectors of the rivers between the USSR and PRC. These unprecedented actions were undertaken by the Chinese authorities at a time when the work of

delivering A.Ya. Pashentsev, chief of the border detachment, and General B.M. Golubev, deputy chief of the border district.

Four trucks came to the Chinese border post, which could have meant the arrival of reserves. Under these conditions, General Golubev thought it necessary to remain at the scene until the conflict was completely resolved. Judging by everything, the Chinese did not see any gain for themselves if they further exacerbated the situation, and the incident concluded with a meeting on Chinese territory. According to Chinese sources, Sun Longzhen, the wife of the shepherd, died in the 10 June incident.

As a result of the skirmish that had taken place, the construction of a new border outpost began. It was called Burgon.

On 13 June, the Government of the USSR issued a declaration (see Appendix IV). The document gave an overview of the history of the establishment of the Russian/USSR and Chinese border, and made a conclusion about the illegality of the Chinese leadership's territorial claims. It also introduced specific proposals for normalising Sino-Soviet relations. The purpose of the declaration was to acquaint both Soviet citizens and the leaders of foreign powers with the position of the Soviet Government. As for the Chinese, addressing them had, to a considerable degree, a political nature, inasmuch as Mao and his entourage knew that the USSR wanted a peaceful resolution of the conflict. And the compilers of the declaration hardly believed that only diplomatic methods would succeed in stopping the provocations on the border. Sooner or later everything would have to be resolved by a demonstration of force. Meanwhile, the Chinese organised the next provocation on Goldinsky Island.

Goldinsky Island (now Bacha Island and part of the PRC) is located on the Amur River (48° 13' 20" northern latitude, 133° 47' 55" eastern longitude), approximately 80 kilometres from Khabarovsk. In 1969 the larger (northwestern) part of Goldinsky belonged to the USSR, and the smaller (southeastern) part belonged to China. The village of Petrovskoye on the Soviet side was located directly across from the island. Territorially, the Soviet part of Goldinsky belonged to the Smidovichsky District of the Jewish Autonomous Region. The area of the island is on the order of 55 square kilometres.

The BM-21 was a truck-mounted multiple rocket launcher with 40 tubes for 122mm calibre rockets. It entered service in the early 1960s and saw its first combat deployment during the Sino-Soviet clashes of March 1969. The complete system – including the Ural-4320 truck with launcher, and 40 rockets, weighing about 14 tones – became known as Grad (Hail) and was usually deployed in batteries of six launchers, six ammunition re-supply trucks (with 80 rockets each), and a battery command post. Together with a battalion headquarters, a headquarters platoon, a maintenance and supply platoon, three batteries usually made an artillery battalion of 18 launchers (capable of delivering 720 rockets in a single volley). (Artwork by David Bocquelet)

Introduced to service in 1961, the T-62 was still a relatively new medium tank when it saw its first combat deployment – against the People's Republic of China during the clashes of 1969. Its primary armament consisted of the 115mm U-5TS smoothbore tank gun with a two-axis stabiliser, and 7.62mm PKT coaxial machine gun (mounted to the right of the main gun). Forty rounds were carried for the main gun with a further 2,500 rounds for the coaxial armament. As of the 1960s, the 12.7mm DShK heavy anti-aircraft gun was optionally mounted on the loader's hatch, but this seems not to have been the case with examples that saw action against China. With its slightly thicker front armour than the older T-54/55 family, it took the Chinese by surprise: unsurprisingly, the example captured during the fighting along the Ussuri River was subjected to extensive studies and strongly influenced the development of new tank-types in the PRC. (Artwork by David Bocquelet)

The ISU-122 was a Soviet-made tank destroyer developed during the closing stages of the Second World War. Essentially, it consisted of the 122mm D-25S gun (with 30 rounds) installed on the chassis of the ISU-152 self-propelled assault gun, protected by a heavily armoured superstructure. Withdrawn from service in the Soviet Army by 1960, it remained one of heaviest anti-tank weapons of the PLA, which received at least six examples left behind by the Soviet Army in Dalian, in Liaoning Province (former Manchuria) after the end of the Second World War. (Artwork by David Bocquelet)

This scout of the Soviet Army is shown wearing winter camouflage overall in white (usually donned atop of the standard M56 uniform) and felt boots. On his back is the R-105M manpack radio, and he is armed with the 7.62x39mm AKM assault rifle. (Artwork by Anderson Subtil)

This soldier of the Soviet Army infantry is shown wearing the standard M56 summer field uniform with SSh-68 steel helmet and tarpaulin jack boots. His gear includes a leather belt with buckle and Y-straps, with 6X4 Type-1 bayonet and ammunition pouch. Atop this he carries a bag for the ShMS gas mask, a bag for hand grenades, and a flask water canteen. His firearm is the 7.62x39mm AKM assault rifle. (Artwork by Anderson Subtil)

The crew of tanks and BTR-60s in Soviet Army units of the 1960s all wore black tank crew overalls (usually atop of the M56 uniform), with standard summer tankers' helmet and tarpaulin jack boots. Their other gear usually included a pouch for a gas mask, while officers and NCOs were armed with a Makarov pistol, usually carried in a leather holster on the belt. (Artwork by Anderson Subtil)

This young, female member of the Red Guard militia is shown wearing her civilian clothes. Her blue jacket might indicate her employment by one of state-owned enterprises. She is shown wearing a Chicom SKS chest pouch, and is armed with the Type-56 SKS semi-automatic rifle. The inset shows the inscription *Hong Wei Bing* (The Red Guards) as printed on that organisation's armbands. (Artwork by Anderson Subtil)

Like the troops that they led at the time, PLA officers generally wore the M-65 uniform. This example is shown with the GK-80 steel helmet and a leather belt also worn by NCOs and private soldiers. Indeed, the only visible difference between officer's uniforms and others was the locally manufactured version of the Tokarev pistol, the open holster for which is shown worn at the waist. (Artwork by Anderson Subtil)

This Chinese infantryman – shown while reading one of the many prints from Leader Mao Zedong's *Red Book* – is illustrated as wearing the M-65 field uniform, with 'Mao' cap and a plastic Red Star, and canvas-topped, rubber-soled footwear (known as 'Liberation Shoes'). His weapon is the Type-56 semi-automatic rifle: the Chinese-made version of the Soviet SKS, distinguishable by its spike bayonet. (Artwork by Anderson Subtil)

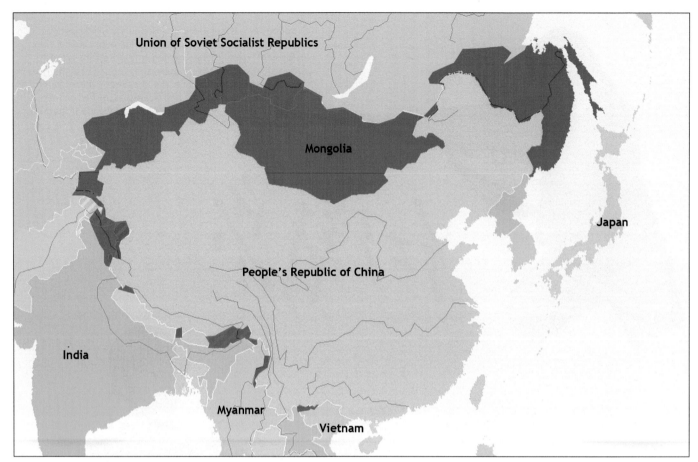

Every Chinese student knows this map. The red colour denotes 'original Chinese territory' – Mongolia, the Russian Far East, Sakhalin. (Map by Tom Cooper based on Chinese Internet)

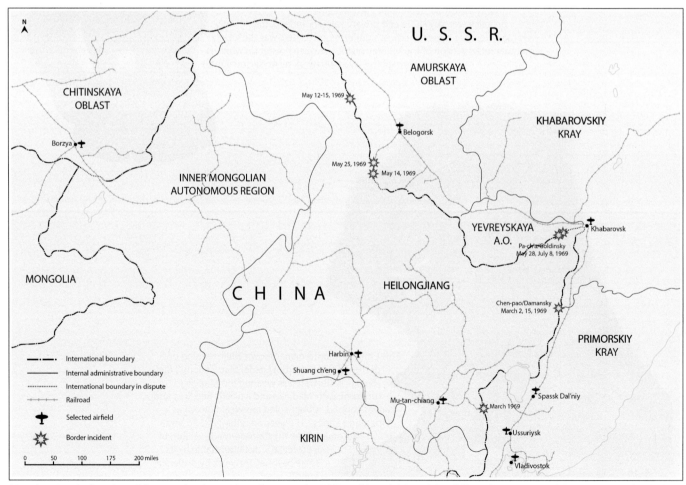

Map showing the location of the 1969 border incidents between the USSR and People's Republic of China (eastern part of the Sino-Soviet border). (Map by George Anderson)

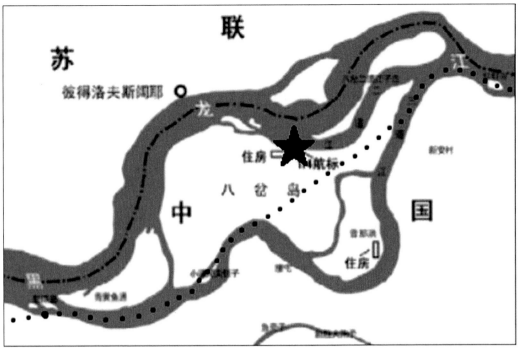

Goldinsky Island on a Chinese map. The current state border is shown by a point-dash line, the border in 1969 is shown by a dotted line (the last one is added to the map by the authors). The star indicates the location of the conflict. (Chinese Internet)

the 15th session of the Joint Sino-Soviet Commission on Shipping was continuing in Khabarovsk. In organising this provocation, the Chinese are deliberately attempting to impede the work of the commission with respect to reaching an approved decision aimed at ensuring the safe passage of ships of both countries on

the Amur and other rivers in their border areas.

The armed attack against the Soviet rivermen, organised by the Chinese authorities on 8 July of this year, is a hostile act and a continuation of provocative Chinese actions on the USSR and PRC border, the responsibility for which completely lies with the Chinese government.

The USSR Ministry of Foreign Affairs lodges a decisive protest with regard to the armed provocation of the Chinese authorities on Goldinsky Island, and demands that the PRC government punish the guilty and immediately take measures so that such actions are not repeated.

For the purpose of protecting their legal rights, the Soviets are forced to take additional measures against the actions of the Chinese authorities, which are aimed at the violation of the state border of the USSR and which present a threat to the security and life of Soviet citizens.

Moscow, 8 July 1969[5]

A short time after the events of Damansky, the Chinese authorities tried to 'absorb' Kirkinsky Island (46° 31′ 37″ northern latitude, 133° 52′ 12″ eastern longitude), located 2.5 kilometres north-northeast of Damansky.

On 20 July 1969, around two companies of PLA soldiers were sent to Kirkinsky, using rafts and boats as means for crossing. Having crossed over to the island, they outfitted trenches and command posts. It is quite probable that the Chinese commanders were placing high hopes on the Soviet decision-making system, where high- and low-ranking chiefs continuously called each other but no one wanted to take any responsibility on himself.

This time, however, an unpleasant surprise awaited the Chinese. The Soviets opened withering fire from mortars and heavy machine guns against the invading violators. Caught by surprise, the Chinese rushed about and tried to hide in the trenches. The mortars reached them even there, and, therefore, they left for their own riverbank. The means for crossing were practically completely destroyed, and as for Chinese casualties, Soviet observers estimated them to be several dozen killed. The following is what Major V.S. Bazhenov, senior officer of 57th Border Detachment's intelligence department, recalled about this:

At the end of July–August, observers at the Kulebyakiny Hills Outpost reported that … about 70 men in civilian clothes, but with weapons, were crossing on boats and rafts to Kirkinsky Island. An operations group from the district's troop directorate, headed by General Major G.P. Sechkin, came to the detachment. After studying the situation, a decision was made not to go to the island and not to engage in battle. The Chinese could set up an ambush similar to the one on 2 March. Fire resources – machine

A. Khandoga, the riverman who was killed. (photo from Aleksandr Leonkin's book, *Bolshoy Ussuriysky Island*, '5 Rim' Publishers, Moscow, in preparation for publication)

guns and a 120mm mortar battery that had been introduced into the detachment's organisation – were brought up to this area. It was proposed to force the violators, using fire, to leave the region.

Before night fell, the Chinese had ostentatiously left the island, but not all of them: 20 men remained. During the day a small group of 5–10 men crossed to the island.

By night, the long-awaited decision on opening fire came, but the troops were strictly prohibited from going to the island. They also had to capture a prisoner. We prepared this operation very carefully, but it was no longer necessary.

On the morning of the third day, the Chinese had hardly begun to cross to the island; they reached the middle of the river, when we started firing from machine guns. They began to panic, many boats overturned, around 3–4 dozen were killed or wounded, and only a small number reached the island. We did not fire when they returned to their riverbank.

The mortar battery, nevertheless, fired some sighting shots at Kirkinsky as a warning and for greater persuasiveness. The Chinese no longer risked crossing to the island during the day; they attempted to do this at night, but even here they were hit. Having understood the complete uselessness of their attempts, they soon after left Kirkinsky in peace.[6]

Some veterans of the 1969 border war now recall that each new report about another conflict on the border produced a feeling that some event was coming that would put an end to this protracted confrontation. There was nothing to do but wait for where and when it would happen.

6

ZHALANASHKOL, 13 AUGUST 1969[1]

The beginning of the 1969 Sino-Soviet border war is usually associated with 2 March 1969, when, as a result of a provocation organised by the Chinese authorities on Damansky Island, dozens of servicemen on both sides died. This conflict also had an end – 13 August, in the area of Lake Zhalanashkol (Kazakh SSR).

This place is located approximately 50 kilometres southwest of the border post in Dulaty, where a confrontation between Soviet and Chinese forces had taken place in May 1969.

Lake Zhalanashkol (the Kazakh word for 'Naked Lake') is located in the northwestern part of the so-called Dzhungarsky Pass (Dzhungarsky Gate). The pass is a flat corridor, with a length of about 80 kilometres and a width of more than 10 kilometres, extending from the northwest to the southeast. The northern entrance to the gate runs into Lake Alakol (Kazakhstan), and the southern entrance into Lake Ebi-Nur (China). The Dzhungarsky Gate separates Dzhungarsky Alatau (in the west) from the Barlyk Range (in the east). Very strong winds are characteristic for the Dzhungarsky Gate: during cold seasons, a southeast wind ('ibe') blows here; sometimes the northwest 'saykan' blows through it.[2]

According to researchers, since ancient times the tribes of Central Asia used the Dzhungarsky Gate to march into Europe. It was namely through here that Genghis Khan's forces passed in their conquest of Central Asia. Part of the principal route of the Great Silk Road was located here.

The part of the border on which the fighting took place was patrolled by the Zhalanashkol Border Outpost (the Eastern Border District's 130th Uch-Aral Border Detachment). This area was considered difficult: in addition to the winds, there were problems with water (it had to be brought in). Some of the soldiers had been sent to the outpost as punishment for misconduct. During the events, Captain N.F. Samokrutov, chief of the outpost, was on leave, and Lieutenant E.B. Govor was in temporary command of the border guards.

As on other sectors of the Sino-Soviet border, tensions in the Lake Zhalanashkol area were created exclusively by the Chinese. Chinese servicemen attempted several times to violate the state border, and these violations became especially more frequent in summer 1969. Organising provocations, the Chinese entered Soviet territory on vehicles and on horseback; unauthorised, they tried to move the border signs and photographed the terrain persistently.

A few days before the battle, Soviet border guards noticed that new people had appeared at the nearest border post (Terekty). The Chinese began to arrive at the borderline, clearly studying the adjacent territory. It had become completely clear that the neighbouring side was planning hostile action.

The scene of the events at Lake Zhalanashkol is marked by the lower star. The upper star indicates the scene of the confrontation at Dulaty. (Authors' drawing)

A day before the battle, a group of Chinese servicemen was photographed 'as a memento'. The majority of the men in the photo died in the 13 August 1969 battle. (Chinese Internet)

Immediately before the events, on 12 August, a border detail, headed by Sergeant Tyukalin, recorded the relocation of a group of Chinese servicemen immediately at the border, in the vicinity of border marker No. 40. In order to pre-empt an exacerbation of the border situation, General M.K. Merkulov, chief of the Eastern Border District, tried to make contact with the Chinese. The Chinese, however, evaded negotiations, which was a clear indication that the plan for initiating an incident had already been implemented and no one intended to revoke it.

Worried by what was happening, the border district command brought the Zhalanashkol Outpost and neighbouring outposts – Rodnikovaya (Bakhtinsky Border District) and 19th Small Cavalry Detachment (Uch-Aral Border Detachment) – to a state of combat readiness. M.F. Liye, the senior officer of the Uch-Aral Border Detachment, and Captain P.S. Terebenkov, assistant chief of staff of the manoeuvre group, were sent to the outpost. Lieutenant Colonel P.I. Nikitenko, chief of staff of the border detachment, who had arrived at the scene of events immediately before the battle, was in charge of the general coordination of the border guards.

Close to midnight, a reinforced detail, headed by Captain Terebenkov, arrived on the left flank, where a secret surveillance post was located. Here the border guards conducted continuous surveillance of the neighbouring side, using technical resources.

On the night of 13 August 1969, several dozen Chinese servicemen covertly advanced 600–700 metres into Soviet territory and settled themselves on Kamennaya Hill and Pravaya Hill. Chinese sources say that the age of the servicemen ranged from 17–37 years of age.

The clothing of the Chinese was the usual PLA summer uniform: cotton jacket and pants, cap with a red star, and sneakers. They were armed with Kalashnikov automatic rifles, SKSs, RPDs, and RPG-2s, and the commanders had TT pistols, everything as it was on Damansky Island. The Chinese had grenades, including antitank grenades (the so-called 'type 3,' an analogue of the Soviet RKG-3

grenade). Some Soviet/Russian authors say that this detachment was part of the special forces; however, the Chinese equipment and their weapons clearly showed that this was a conventional subunit, consisting of infantry and border guards. Fang Jinzhong, an infantry company commander, directed the actions of the main Chinese group.

At around 04:00 a.m., local Soviet time, a border detail consisting of Junior Sergeant Dulepov and Private Yegortsev set off for the Kamennaya Hill area. The detail discovered the Chinese, which Dulepov immediately reported to the outpost. A few minutes later, another detail, headed by Junior Sergeant Babichev, discovered another group of Chinese near Pravaya Hill.

Lieutenant Govor raised the alarm at the outpost, after which he left for the scene of the border violation. Captain Terebenkov also came here. The officers personally observed the Chinese on Kamennaya Hill, and also the movement of other groups of Chinese.

At this time, Junior Lieutenant V.V. Puchkov, platoon leader of a motorised manoeuvre group, was at the neighbouring outpost of 19th Small Cavalry Detachment. Three APCs were under his command. An assault group of 30 border guards, led by Senior Lieutenant V.F. Olshevsky, deputy chief of Uch-Aral Border Detachment's Dzhungarsky Outpost, was biding its time in the APCs. At the command of Captain Chudinov, the detachment's operations duty officer, Puchkov's APCs moved double time to the Zhalanashkol Outpost. It was namely they who accepted battle on the border.

Motorised manoeuvre groups from the Uch-Aral and Bakhtinsky Border Detachments were also sent to the Zhalanashkol Border Outpost. In truth, they arrived in time for the end of the battle.

Before dawn the Soviet border guards, who were located at the command and surveillance post (Skalistaya Hill), conducted surveillance of the enemy. The Chinese positions not only on Soviet territory, but also behind the borderline were recorded. The Soviets

Fang Jinzhong with his son. The photo was taken shortly before the events. (Chinese Internet)

estimated the total number of PLA soldiers who took part in the action at 150–170 men, of whom 70–80 were directly on USSR territory. According to contemporary Chinese information, 122 servicemen took part in the operation; that being said, however, it is not known if they have in mind all participants in the battle or only those who infiltrated into Soviet territory (some Chinese sources say that more than 100 servicemen crossed the border).

Information about the border violation was quickly sent to Eastern Border District headquarters. General Lieutenant Merkulov immediately communicated with Moscow, with the operations duty officer of the KGB's Main Directorate of Border Guards. The latter tried to obtain clear instructions from the leadership, but none of the generals in the capital wanted to take on further responsibility (judging by everything, the Moscow generals had not learned the Damansky lesson). Seeing that Moscow was of little use, Merkulov switched over to communications with the border detachment at the scene.

A helicopter that was at the disposal of the border guards flew over the hills and confirmed the presence of Chinese servicemen on Soviet territory. The latter did not react at all to the appearance of the helicopter, but cameramen among them began to film its flight.

Before the beginning of the operation to drive the Chinese back beyond the borderline, Lieutenant Colonel Nikitenko formed up all personnel (around 50 men) and specified the tasks for each group of border guards. He made it clear that the preferred variant was the peaceful withdrawal of the Chinese from the positions they occupied. If they opened fire, however, then the border guards were to act decisively and accordingly as the situation warranted.

Using a loudspeaker and a special Russian–Chinese phrasebook, Lieutenant Govor, who was at the command and surveillance post, demanded several times that the Chinese leave Soviet territory and warned about responsibility in case of further hostile actions. As usual, there was no answer.

At 07:15 a group of 12 Chinese soldiers crossed the border from the direction of the Terekty Border Post and set off for the northeast slope of Kamennaya Hill. On the order from Lieutenant Colonel Nikitenko, APC No. 217, under the command of Lieutenant Puchkov, moved in the direction of the Chinese, with the intention

of driving them from Soviet territory without using weapons. Some distance behind it, APC No. 218, in which an assault team under the command of Captain Terebenkov was located, moved. Olshevsky's group moved in dismounted formation in the direction of the left part of Kamennaya Hill. Govor's group moved to Pravaya Hill from the right flank, covered by the armour of APC No. 220 (see Sketch Map 5).

Apparently having taken the manoeuvre of the APCs as the commencement of an attack, the Chinese opened fire. Puchkov, implementing the operations plan that had been developed earlier, answered with the same. After this, Govor's, Terebenkov's, and Olshevsky's groups shifted to dynamic operations to kill the Chinese.

Puchkov's APC went around Kamennaya Hill on the left and the assault group disembarked. The border guards deployed in extended order and attacked the hill. APC No. 217, manoeuvring, fired at the Chinese who were located on the hill and near the border. APC No. 218 also fired at the Chinese. After a few minutes of fighting, Terebenkov's group disembarked from it on the left flank of Kamennaya Hill.

Having managed to get closer to the left part of Kamennaya Hill, Olshevsky's group began to exchange fire with the Chinese, who had entrenched themselves on the hill. The border guards went to ground, awaiting the command to attack.

The border guards of Govor's group forced down some Chinese (as many as 10 men) from the neighbouring Pravaya Hill, after which the former took up a convenient position to conduct fire against both Kamennaya Hill and the Chinese reserves, who were trying to help the Chinese on Kamennaya Hill (see Sketch Map 6).

P.S. Terebenkov recalls the following:

When we were ordered to attack, the soldiers immediately got out of the APC and, dispersing, ran to the hill at intervals of 6–7 metres. The Chinese were firing not only from Kamennaya, but also from the borderline. I had a light machine gun. Noticing a small hillock, I laid down behind it and shot several bursts at the trenches. At this time the soldiers had made a dash. After they went to ground and opened automatic fire, I started to run. In this way we supported one another and moved.[3]

E. Govor recalls how they managed to liberate Pravaya Hill:

I commanded one of the groups in the battle. We circled Pravaya Hill and attacked it. There were fewer Maoists here than on Kamennaya. Supported by an armoured personnel carrier, we quickly dealt with them. From Pravaya there was a good view of Kamennaya's crest and the trenches with the Maoists in them. We set up the machine guns and struck them.[4]

Having lost control of Pravaya Hill, the Chinese tried to organise an all-round defence on Kamennaya Hill. However, fire from the heavy machine guns that had been set up on the APCs made it impossible for them to conduct aimed fire against the attacking border guards. The latter were able to move close to the top of the hill, after which they launched grenades.

Terebenkov witnessed the following:

After Olshevsky was wounded, I took command of his group as well. Grenades flew from the crest of Kamennaya. Black with white handles. One fell nearby and exploded. I was wounded in the hand and head. Kirpichev from Olshevsky's group ran to help me. The soldier bandaged my head, and I bandaged my hand

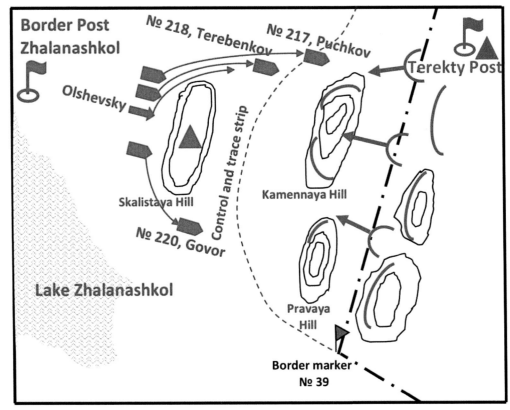

Sketch Map 5: Deployment of the sides immediately before the beginning of the shooting on 13 August 1969. (Map by authors)

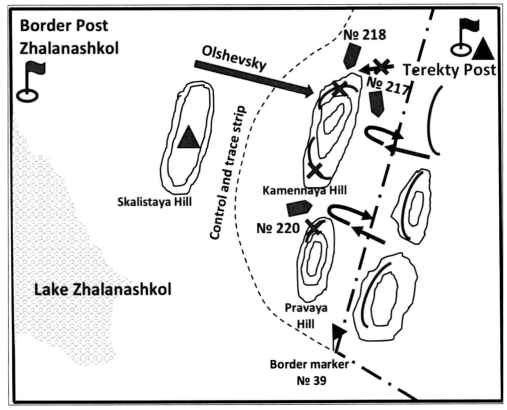

Sketch Map 6: Battle on 13 August 1969. (Map by authors)

No. 217 had been pierced several times, and he had been wounded in the thigh. The junior lieutenant bandaged himself and continued to fight. A bullet struck Pishchulev, the APC driver, in the right hand, after which he then drove the vehicle with his left hand. When the turret jammed, Puchkov brought the APC to the starting point. After this he moved into one of the APCs from the neighbouring Bakhtinsky Border Detachment and once again advanced to the hills, preventing the Chinese reinforcements from crossing the borderline.

Two groups of Chinese servicemen tried to help their dying comrades, but they were beaten back. The most intensive part of the battle ended 65 minutes after it had begun (75 minutes after, according to Chinese information).

The reserves – manoeuvre groups from the Uch-Aral and Bakhtinsky Detachments – arrived for the end of the battle. Having deployed on Kamennaya Hill, they used their fire to suppress the attempt by the Chinese to move up their reserves. The shooting finally stopped around midday.

On this same day the USSR MFA handed a note to the PRC MFA with a description of what had happened on the border, and lodged a protest:

Note from the USSR MFA to the PRC Ministry of Foreign Affairs
The Ministry of Foreign Affairs of the Union of Soviet Socialist Republics declares the following to the Ministry of Foreign Affairs of the People's Republic of China.

Since the beginning of May of this year and through the present time, the Chinese authorities have been deliberately exacerbating the situation on the Sino-Soviet border in the area of the Semipalatinsk *Oblast* of the Kazakh SSR, systematically organising confrontational incursions into Soviet territory. In its notes dated 4 May and 11 June 1969, the USSR MFA demanded that the Chinese authorities stop escalating the tensions on the border in the above-mentioned area. The Chinese, however, have not heeded this.

On 13 August of this year, at 7:40 (local time), several groups of Chinese servicemen violated the Soviet state border ten kilometres

myself. I wanted to glance at my watch – it wasn't there. The metal watchband had been broken by a grenade fragment. I then found it. The hands showed 8:10.[5]

During the subsequent analysis of the battle, the actions of Junior Lieutenant Vladimir Puchkov were especially appreciated. His APC east of the populated area of Zhalanashkol (Semipalatinsk Obl.) and moved further into Soviet territory. Despite warning signals and a demand that they leave USSR territory, the violators not only continued to remain on Soviet territory, but also opened machine-gun fire against Soviet border guards. After the Soviet border guards took measures to interdict the criminal actions of the Soviet border violators, the Chinese attempted to bring up 2 more groups, numbering 60-70 men.

As a result of the measures taken by the Soviet border guards, the border violators were driven back beyond the borderlines; that being said, two Chinese servicemen were detained on Soviet territory. There were several killed and wounded.

The facts irrefutably attest that the armed provocation by the Chinese authorities on the Sino-Soviet border were planned in advance this time as well. On 12 August, the day before the battle, Soviet border guard observers discovered that military subunits had been brought up from the Chinese side of the border in this sector, reinforced groups of servicemen had been relocated, and work had been done to set up lines of communication. To prevent the situation from becoming more difficult, the Soviet border authorities called for a meeting with a representative from the PRC border guard. The latter, however, declined the meeting.

With regard to this new armed provocation on the Sino-Soviet border, the USSR Ministry of Foreign Affairs is lodging a strong protest to the PRC Ministry of Foreign Affairs and demands that an end be put to the violations of the border of the Soviet Union and to the armed provocations against Soviet border guards.

Once again the Soviets warn that any breach into the territory of the Soviet Union will be decisively repelled. All responsibility for any serious consequences of the Chinese provocations on the Sino-Soviet border rests with the government of the PRC.

Moscow, 13 August 1969.[6]

The Chinese also responded, with a note having similar content:

To the Embassy of the USSR in China:
On the morning of August 13, 1969, the Soviet side sent two helicopters, dozens of tanks and armoured vehicles and several hundred armed troops to intrude into the Tiehliekti area in Yumin County of the Sinkiang Uighur Autonomous Region, China, who penetrated a depth of two kilometres, unwarrantedly fired at the Chinese frontier guards on normal patrol duty, killing and wounding many of them on the spot, and closed in on them. Driven beyond the limits of forbearance, the Chinese frontier guards were compelled to fight back in self-defence. At present, the Soviet side is continuing to amass large numbers of troops and tanks in an attempt to provoke still larger armed conflicts; the situation is developing.

The Chinese Government hereby lodges a strong protest with the Soviet Government against its deliberate intrusion into Chinese territory and provocation of a fresh incident of bloodshed, and demands that the Soviet Government immediately withdraw all its intruding troops from Chinese territory and immediately stop its firing. Otherwise, the Soviet Government must be held fully responsible for all the grave consequences arising therefrom.

Ministry of Foreign Affairs of
The People's Republic of China
Peking, August 13, 1969[7]

In the 13 August 1969 battle, the Soviets lost two killed – Junior Sergeant M. Dulepov and Private V. Ryazanov. The following was the official information about these two deaths:

Junior Sergeant Mikhail Konstantinovich Dulepov, dog service instructor (130th Border Detachment's 14th "Zhalanashkol" Border Outpost), born in 1948, Russian, Komsomol member, native of the village of Sylva, Perm District, Perm *Oblast*; conscripted into active military service on 21 June 1967 by the Perm Regional Military Commissariat. Awarded the Order of the Red Star (posthumously).

Private Vitaly Pavlovich Ryazanov, radio and telegraph operator (130th Border Detachment's 13th "19th Siding" Border Outpost), born in 1949, Russian, Komsomol member, native of the town of Zlatoust, Chelyabinsk *Oblast*; conscripted into active military service on 31 October 1968 by the Zlatoust Regional Military Commissariat. Awarded the Order of the Red Star (posthumously).

Thirty men were wounded (including Captain Terebenkov, Senior Lieutenant Olshevsky, Junior Lieutenant Puchkov, Sergeant Isachkov, Sergeant Ovchinnikov, Corporal Pishchulev, Private Kirpichev, Private Shekhovtsov, and others).

After the battle, the Soviet border guards removed the bodies of the dead Chinese from the battlefield. Two of them had professional imported movie cameras. The developed film confirmed how events had specifically developed on the battlefield (some of the photos are available on the Internet). In addition, on the night of 14 August the Soviet border guards observed how the Chinese had carried off around a dozen of their dead, who had been lying between Kamennaya Hill and the borderline, to their own territory. According to contemporary Chinese information, 29 Chinese servicemen had died in the 13 August battle, including Wen Binglin (cameraman from the Central Studio of News and Documentary Films), Li Liangxiang (cameraman from the 1 August Film Studio), and Wang Yibing (reporter from Xinhua News Agency), and 39 others had been wounded.

The following is the complete list of Chinese who died at Lake Zhalanashkol on 13 August 1969: Pei Yingzhang, Li Guozhen, Gao Chunling, Li Liangxiang, Cao Xinlong, Yi Zhongxuan, Guo Yufeng, Liu Yunzeng, Li Guichang, Jing Changxiang, Wang Mingyuan, Fang Jinzhong, Ding Xinnian, Yuan Guozhen, He Zongyi, Li Tiangao, Yang Shihuai, Zhang Keri, Li Ruizeng, Li Jian, Wen Binglin, Wang Yibing, You Changan, Zhang Jili, Liu Yixin, Wang Chengzhen, Yin Qingqi, Wang Yongchen, Yang Zhenglin.

Some Chinese publications cite other figures for those who died in the 13 August 1969 battle (most often 38); however, these citations are not supported by lists of names, and, therefore, cannot be considered reliable.

The heavy Chinese losses are explained by the fact that from the moment the shooting began, the Soviet border guards were set up to uncompromisingly suppress the enemy, not simply push him out of Soviet territory. The Soviet veterans who directly participated in the events draw this conclusion: the reason was the outrage the border guards felt toward the Maoists after the 2 March events on the Ussuri River.

There were no documents on the dead Chinese; however, one of them had a curious badge with an image of Mao Zedong and the inscription: 'Awarded to commemorate the victorious repelling of the aggression by the Soviet revisionists on Zhenbao Island. Made in the Shenyang region.' Some Russian authors concluded from

Corporal V. Shcherbina receives the automatic weapon of deceased M. Dulepov. (Military Museum of Hanoi, via Albert Grandolini)

Wen Binglin. (Chinese Internet)

Private Vladimir Zavarnitsyn reads a letter from home. In the 13 August 1969 battle he personally killed a Chinese grenade thrower who was attempting to damage a Soviet APC. (Military Museum of Hanoi, via Albert Grandolini)

Li Liangxiang. (Chinese Internet)

this that the dead man had some relation to the March battles on Damansky (Zhenbao) Island. Moreover, he had been specially sent to the area of the Dzhungarsky Gate as one who had experience in organising provocations on the border. There are two reasons, however, that make this conclusion doubtful:

1. If the badge had been made in 'Shenyang region,' then it clearly was not an official award. Most likely, some servicemen from the Shenyang Military District had hurried to commemorate their participation in the events on Damansky by the local production of a badge, even if it did not have particular relevance to what had happened.

2. Individual Chinese sources give some information, albeit scanty, about all the men who died at Lake Zhalanashkol – the year and place of birth, year of conscription and year they joined the CPC, etc. If any of them had taken part in the battles on Damansky, this would

probably have been made known, naturally with a proclamation of heroism, self-sacrifice, etc. However, there is not a word about this.

A report came up on the Chinese Internet that the dead cameramen had been involved in the filming on Damansky; however, the nature of this involvement was not made clear – whether they were there or whether they looked at the shots that others had taken. It is possible that someone had received this badge as a souvenir.

Many Soviet/Russian publications mention three wounded Chinese who were captured; allegedly, one survived and the other two died from their severe wounds. It is true that now the Soviet veterans who directly participated in the battle and witnesses cannot precisely say how many Chinese were captured. Chinese sources – citing the survivor – state with complete confidence that not three, but four soldiers were captured. Those who died of their wounds were cameraman Wen Binglin, Jing Changxiang, and Pei Yingzhang (the latter headed the group that tried to drive out Puchkov before the shooting started). Eyewitnesses say that the surviving Chinese soldier (Yuan Guoxiao, who was 17 years old) was in a state of extreme stress immediately after being wounded: having been allowed to bandage himself, from time to time he hysterically

Soviet border guards on Kamennaya Hill. (Military Museum of Hanoi, via Albert Grandolini)

Chinese weapons found on the battlefield. (Military Museum of Hanoi, via Albert Grandolini)

shouted out some slogans. Subsequently, he recovered in a hospital with wounded Soviet soldiers.

The border guards found automatic rifles, carbines, light machine guns, several pistols, grenades, rounds, a radio set, etc. on the battlefield.

Inasmuch as the Chinese did not show any initiative with regard to having the bodies of those who died returned, it was decided to bury them near the border. The bodies of 19 dead soldiers were placed in coffins that had been crudely hammered together from boards and buried on Soviet territory. A photo of the dead man and an appropriate certificate were placed in each coffin.

On 18 September 1969, per an agreement with the Chinese authorities, the coffins with the dead bodies were dug up and sent to the Chinese.

In his recollections of the Zhalanashkol events, I.I. Petrov, former political officer of the Eastern Border District, described

this episode as follows, citing unnamed witnesses:

Their bodies, which were taken immediately to the scene of the transfer at the border, were literally dropped in a pit on the neighbouring side, which had been prepared beforehand; the pit was covered with dirt and flattened to the level of the ground, and the coffins in which the bodies of the dead provocateurs had been transferred were gathered and burned in a bonfire. As for the prisoner who was transferred, he changed his clothes right at the border, and threw the clothes he had been wearing into the fire. He was kicked into a closed vehicle.[8]

Chinese sources confirm the fact of the burning of the coffins, but, that being said, point out that the remains of the dead were transported to and buried in a memorial cemetery, with all fitting honours.

These same sources say that it was practically impossible to identify the bodies, inasmuch as an entire month had lapsed since the battle and it was a very hot time of the year.

The Chinese had been informed about the prisoner; however, his name was not known for some time, since Yuan Guoxiao was silent at the interrogations. Some time later he gave an assumed name (Li), which was reported to the local Chinese authorities. As a result, right up until the time of Yuan Guoxiao's return, the Chinese mistakenly assumed that a completely different soldier had survived from the group that had died.

The prisoner was transferred to the Chinese on 22 September. As Yuan Guoxiao himself now recalls, they dressed him in civilian clothing and reported that he could return to China. On the Chinese side, military physicians met the prisoner. He was examined and clothed in a new uniform, after which he was brought in an ambulance to a rally.

In China, applause and cheering awaited Yuan Guoxiao. Several days later, he addressed a large meeting of servicemen, where he gave a speech (more precisely, he read a text that political officers had prepared for him). A notable fact was that the text called his imprisonment a kidnapping, inasmuch as the PLA considered being captured a disgrace.

For two months Yuan Guoxiao met with high-ranking officers and addressed meetings and rallies. He then served another two years in the army, after which he requested to be demobilised in order to help his parents on their farm. This request was met.

However, in his hometown in Henan Province, he was not met with special enthusiasm. Voices began to be heard that denounced Yuan Guoxiao. They said that, having been a Soviet prisoner, he could be on the path of treason. He was also reproached that all his comrades had died, but he had survived. Some time later, however, all accusations were dropped. Yuan Guoxiao is now a successful businessman, involved with the chili pepper trade, and he meets with young border guards. It is difficult to verify his recollections; however, some details he recalls about being in a Soviet prison are

18 September 1969. The Chinese take away the bodies of the dead PLA soldiers. (Chinese Internet)

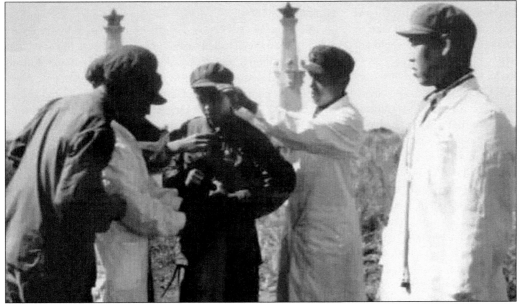

Military physicians examine Yuan Guoxiao, after which he was brought to a rally, 22 September 1969. (Chinese Internet)

quite curious. For example, he says that at first a military interpreter who spoke with a Russian accent, communicated with him. Then another interpreter, a Chinese named Zhan, appeared, who said that he was from Shandong Province.

A Chinese publication stated that on the day Yuan Guoxiao returned to the PRC, a conversation was held between Soviet and Chinese representatives about the fact that the bodies of two servicemen – soldier Wang Yongchen and Deputy Company Commander Yang Zhenglin – had not yet been found. The Soviets permitted the Chinese to search for the dead men on Soviet territory. On that day – 22 September – the remains of Wang Yongchen, and some time later those of Yang Zhenglin, were found and taken away.

An investigation group created by the PRC Central Military Commission studied what had happened at Lake Zhalanashkol. According to available information, around 100 responsible individuals were interrogated. Nothing is known about the commission's conclusions, but, in any case, after the events of 13 August the Chinese no longer tried to seize sectors on Soviet territory. This was treated in the USSR as evidence that the battle at Lake Zhalanashkol convinced the Chinese leadership that from that time on, any and all provocations on the border would be interdicted with the maximum possible force. At that time the Chinese press did not report anything about that conflict, possibly because the country's leadership acknowledged that it was not desirable to inform the population about the defeat, especially since several months before these events Chinese propaganda had been trumpeting about 'a victory' on Zhenbao Island. Contemporary

Chinese publications acknowledge the complete rout of the PLA detachment at Lake Zhalanashkol; that being said, they express the opinion that the Chinese soldiers were poorly trained and did not have the necessary weapons to fight Soviet APCs, that they were not given timely support, etc. They also say that Soviet T-62 tanks and around 300 soldiers took part in the battle: neither statement is true. It is noteworthy that the concept of an unsuccessful action on the border is not explained or discussed. The goal of the operation

was possibly to make a propaganda film that demonstrated the heroism of PLA soldiers fighting against the 'Soviet revisionists'. Some Chinese publications say that a large group of journalists and cameramen (as many as 20 men) had come earlier to the scene of the events, which speaks in favour of the above-mentioned assumption. Everyone miscalculated – both those who planned the provocation and those who tried to implement it. The latter paid for the Zhalanashkol venture with their young lives.

7
WHAT THEY FOUGHT WITH ON THE BORDER[1]

Briefly stated, in the battles on the Sino-Soviet border in 1969, Soviet weapons of Soviet production opposed Soviet weapons of Chinese production, or, to put it another way, Soviet weapons of the 1960s opposed Soviet weapons of the 1950s. In no way, however, did this mean that the Chinese were at a flagrant disadvantage in a technical respect. The fact is, Soviet military designers always worked with an eye on the future; therefore, they developed models that would not become obsolete for decades.

The principal personal weapons for the Chinese troops were the Kalashnikov automatic rifle (AK-47) and the Simonov semi-automatic carbine (SKS-45) (the numbers in parentheses indicate the year they were adopted).[2] The popularity of the AK-47 had long ago transcended all possible national boundaries. One need only mention that the AK-47 reflected a definite military idea, the essence of which lay in the necessity of furnishing infantry subunits with cheap, simple, and reliable weapons. It was namely these demands that the Second World War presented, and Soviet designers quickly accomplished the assigned task.

The shortcomings and advantages of M.T. Kalashnikov's creation are well known. Among the former were the lack of a high degree of accuracy of rounds fired at mid and long ranges, the recoil, an angle of incline of the rifle butt that was too great in relation to the axis of the barrel, and the inconvenient location of the safety/change lever. In general, it must be said that, with regard to individual characteristics, the weapon was of rather average quality: its rate of fire, range, weight, magazine capacity, etc. were not particularly outstanding.

In one respect, however, the AK-47 was an unsurpassable weapon: its reliability, the most important quality of a firearm, in comparison with which everything else pales. The AK-47 was exceptionally reliable, and this meant that it fired in water and sand, under conditions of heat or mechanical pressure, in winter's cold and in summer's heat. The secret of the AK-47's reliability and that of its modifications was in the very design of the weapon's operation. This design was based on the release of part of the gunpowder gases and their powerful effects into the piston. To this must be added the size of the moving parts and the quite considerable gaps between them and the barrel casing – hence the reliability. Naturally, such construction adversely affected the precision of fire; however, counting on reliability justified itself.

It was namely this reliability and simplicity, together with the remaining characteristics, average though they might have been, that made the AK-47 a truly outstanding invention. A large army armed with these automatic weapons was a deadly danger for the enemy.

Of course, during the time of the 'cultural revolution' in China it was prohibited to even mention the name 'Kalashnikov.' They came up with a simple solution: name the copied Soviet weapons by numbers. Thus, in the Chinese classification the AK-47 became the faceless 'Type 56.'

This 'Type 56' was opposed in the border clashes by the Soviet AKM – the modernised Kalashnikov (*avtomat Kalashnikova modernizirovannyi*), which was adopted in 1959. The latter differed from its predecessor basically in its technical aspects. The AKM had a lighter punched barrel casing, an improved firing and trigger mechanism (with a delay in the operating cycle of the hammer), and a more comfortable rifle butt. Practically speaking, the AKM basically did not differ from the AK-47.

The SKS-45 carbine was adopted into the Soviet Army at about the same time as the AK-47. The former could shoot somewhat farther and more accurately than the latter; however, the SKS-45 created a substantially smaller density of fire. For some time the Soviet rifle subunits had both the automatic weapon and the carbine, which created certain inconveniences. Gradually the combat qualities of the automatic weapon were improved, and this led to a wide-scale replacement of the SKS-45 by the AK-47. For some time the carbines remained in air defence units, but eventually they were taken out of the weapons inventory. At present, the SKS-45 is used for formal events in honour guard companies.

A Chinese patrol in the area of Damansky Island. The soldier walking in front is armed with an AK-47; the soldier on the right is carrying an SKS-45 on his shoulder. (Military Museum of Hanoi, via Albert Grandolini)

A Soviet border guard armed with an AKM, Nizhne-Mikhaylovka Border Outpost. (Military Museum of Hanoi, via Albert Grandolini)

As for the Chinese infantry, in 1969 it was copying Soviet rifle units of the mid-1950s, that is, it had both AK-47s and SKS-45s. Models of these weapons may be seen in the Central Border Museum of the Russian Federal Security Service (FSB); on display here are an AK-47 No. 5262524 and a SKS-45 No. X9957, captured at Damansky. Next to them is a Chinese-manufactured TT pistol (Tula, Tokarev), which was found on the island after one of the skirmishes that took place before 2 March 1969. It would be interesting to establish, according to the number of the pistol (No. 3205515), to which of the Chinese commanders it belonged and under what circumstances it was lost.

Of the three above-mentioned models, two (the automatic weapon and the pistol) were manufactured in China, while the carbine was manufactured in the USSR. This fact clearly demonstrates how paradoxically, at times, relationships develop in the so-called socialist camp.

The principal light machine gun used by the Chinese was the Degtyarev light machine gun (*ruchnoy pulemet Degtyareva*/RPD) – 'Type 56-1' according to its Chinese classification. It appeared as part of the armaments of the Soviet Army at the same time as the SKS-45 and AK-47. Later it was replaced by the more modern Kalashnikov light machine gun (*ruchnoy pulemet Kalashnikova*/RPK), which Soviet soldiers used on the border.

As for the comparative characteristics of the RPD and RPK, they were very similar. The RPD was somewhat heavier and it had belt feeding. The RPK was handier in subunits armed with AKMs, inasmuch as these weapons had the same designer – M.T. Kalashnikov. Strictly speaking, there were not many differences between the AKM and RPK. The machine gun had a long barrel and prop, a magazine with greater capacity, and a device that made it possible to take into account lateral wind. Many parts of the RPK and AKM were generally interchangeable, which created obvious conveniences.

Among the shortcomings of the RPK were its range, which was not particularly long with respect to being able to conduct precision fire, and the inconvenient location of the safety/change lever. In principle, it was very similar to the AKM: high reliability at the expense of precision at long ranges.

An important detail was the fact that the ammunition for all the above-enumerated weapons – the machine gun, the automatic weapon, and the carbine – was supplied by the same model rounds. These rounds – 7.62x39mm – had been invented during the Second World War and are still being used.

In addition to the RPD, during the border fighting the Chinese used the Goryunov SG-43 medium machine gun ('Type 53/57'). For example, in one of the Chinese documentaries about events on Damansky there are several cadres forming a machine gun team with this weapon: one soldier is firing while a second is feeding the belt. Judging from the surrounding terrain, this machine gun was set up on the Chinese bank of the Ussuri River for infantry support.

Externally, the SG-43 was very similar to the well-known 'Maxim,' only with air cooling. A characteristic feature of the Goryunov machine gun was the circular mount. The SG-43

Shortly before the battle at Lake Zhalanashkol. The seated Chinese soldier is armed with a Degtyarev ('Type 56-1') light machine gun. The soldier standing on the right is armed with an AK; the one on the left is armed with an SKS. (Military Museum of Hanoi, via Albert Grandolini)

This photo was taken during the conflict on Damansky. In the foreground is a Soviet soldier armed with an RPK; behind him is a grenade launcher with an RPG-7. (Military Museum of Hanoi, via Albert Grandolini)

distinguished itself as a very reliable and powerful weapon; its great weight and unwieldiness, however, made it not very convenient.

Some researchers into the events on the Sino-Soviet border mistakenly associate the Chinese SG-43 with the category of high-calibre [heavy] machine guns. In fact, the ammunition supply for this machine gun was the usual 7.62mm rifle rounds.

In the fighting on 2 March 1969, Soviet border troops used only the Kalashnikov automatic weapon, the APC turret machine guns,

One of those cadres with Chinese SG-43 medium machine gun ('Type 53/57'). (Chinese Internet)

A Chinese soldier with an RPG-2 on Damansky Island, 1969. (Chinese Internet)

too. They had no grenades, and this circumstance resulted in casualties that could have been avoided: had the Soviet soldiers had this simple but powerful weapon, more undoubtedly would have survived, even taking into account that the Chinese attack was a surprise.

After the first battle the Soviet border troops received F-1 defensive grenades and RGD-5 offensive grenades. The dispersion of the latter's shrapnel did not exceed 20 metres; therefore, enemy soldiers were only hit if the grenade was thrown 40–45 metres. The F-1, better known as 'the lemon,' had a somewhat greater range, about 30–35 metres (true, in many manuals it was written that the dispersion of its shrapnel could be as much as 200 metres, but this occurred extremely rarely).

The Chinese had grenades that externally resembled elongated cylinders with wooden handles.

As is known, Chinese troops made wide use of the RPG-2 grenade launcher in the fighting on Damansky. This grenade launcher was, in fact, an improved variation of the German 'Panzerfaust' (or, as the heroes of some Soviet war films sometimes incorrectly named it, the 'Faustpatron'). By today's standards this weapon was rather poor: in the absence of a telescopic sight, the range was all of 150 metres. As experienced riflemen say, it was practically impossible to hit a moving target with an RPG-2 at distances greater than 100 metres. Nevertheless, at short distances this grenade launcher was very dangerous, and its hollow-charge grenade easily damaged armoured transports and infantry fighting vehicles.

The RPG-7 grenade launcher, which was part of the weapon inventory of Soviet subunits, was a much more powerful weapon. Its range was 300 metres, made possible by the presence of a telescopic sight. Today the RPG-7 is used in the Russian Army, and with its continuous improvements there is no way it will become obsolete.

As part of their armaments the Soviet border troops also had the SPG-9 antitank rocket launcher, a recoilless gun. The ammunition for the SPG-9 was the 73mm antitank rocket with tail vanes, which could penetrate armour with thickness of up to 400 millimetres. It took four soldiers to carry the rocket launcher and two to operate it in battle. The Chinese also had SPG-9-type rocket launchers, but they were earlier models than their Soviet counterparts.

In the fighting on the border the Soviet border troops used the BTR-60PB APC, which was adopted in 1965.[3] The BTR-60PB was an eight-wheeled vehicle that could transport nine riflemen. Infantrymen could fire directly from the APC through ports (three on each side of the chassis). The APC's main weapon was the KPVT machine gun (14.5mm calibre) and, paired with it, the PKT machine gun (7.62mm).

The combat use of the APCs assumed their following behind tanks and extended infantry lines. In the 1969 battles, however, everything looked completely different, inasmuch as the fighting took place in a small area and under quite specific conditions. In

Private Petr Tirchenko with an RPG-7 grenade launcher, Damansky Island region, 1969. (Military Museum of Hanoi, via Albert Grandolini)

fact, the APCs assumed the role of tanks, attacking the enemy in the front line.

The motorised rifle subunits of 199th Regiment, which took part in the fighting on Damansky, also had APCs, but theirs were an earlier model – the BTR-60P. This vehicle lacked a turret and was completely open on top, and instead of a high-calibre machine gun it had only one 7.62mm machine gun. The machine gunners were in no way protected and stood up to their waists above the assault section.

The replacement of the BTR-60P with the more modern BTR-60PB occurred when the shortcomings of the former were recognised. Even during the Second World War it became clear that an APC that was open at the top was extremely vulnerable under urban conditions. Later on, this was confirmed several times, for example, during the events in Hungary (1956) and Czechoslovakia (1968), as well as during the war in Vietnam.

In the battles of 15 March (Damansky) and 13 August (Zhalanashkol), APCs were used for both the delivery of infantry to the dismount area and as individual pieces of armoured equipment. Losses in APCs were basically explained by the not always completely correct use of these vehicles; Soviet commanders, however, consciously accepted this as the situation developed.

In addition to this, the fighting confirmed the high degree of survivability of Soviet APCs. It turned out that the design of a multi-wheeled vehicle with a hull floor that rose high above the ground was correct. The presence of several wheels made it possible to maintain the speed of the APC under conditions of repeated damage to the running gear, while the large gap between the ground and the hull floor ensured, in case the APC ran over a mine, a partial reduction of the energy of the explosion.

As is known, the Soviets used the T-62 tank in the 15 March fighting. At first, Colonel D.V. Leonov made an unsuccessful raid into a channel of the Ussuri River; then a group of tanks took part in the fighting directly on the island.

The T-62 was a development of its famous predecessor, the T-55, which was known as a reliable 'workhorse' in many wars and conflicts. The principal innovation of the T-62 was the smoothbore 115mm U5-TS cannon (the 'Hammer') paired with a machine gun. This cannon made it possible for the shell to attain a high initial velocity and, consequently, strike a target by direct laying at a great distance. Inasmuch as the barrel channel had no rifling, the steadiness of the shell in flight was ensured by control fins. Another important innovation of the T-62 was the cannon stabilisation unit in the vertical and horizontal planes (the 'Meteor'), which made it possible to fire even while the tank was moving on rough terrain. Nevertheless, the T-62 did not completely justify the hopes that the military had for it. Indicative was the fact that production of the T-62 ceased earlier than its predecessor's (the T-55).

In the fighting, the Chinese, practically speaking, did not use armoured equipment. Nevertheless, the Soviet command did not discount this possibility and, therefore, took necessary measures. For example, on 15 March, the border troops at the Nizhne-Mikhaylovka Outpost were armed with grenades in case Chinese tanks appeared.

Some Soviet veterans of the events recall that the Chinese did make one attempt to use armour. The incident involved four self-propelled ISU-122

The Chinese SPG-9-type rocket launchers near Damansky. (Military Museum of Hanoi, via Albert Grandolini)

13 August 1969, Lake Zhalanashkol area. Soviet BTR-60PBs after the battle. (Military Museum of Hanoi, via Albert Grandolini)

Damansky region. In the background – Soviet BTR-60P. The radio operator is armed with an AKM with a drum magazine. These magazines, which hold 75 rounds, were designated for RPK light machine guns; they could, however, be used for AKMs as well. (Military Museum of Hanoi, via Albert Grandolini)

Speaking about the M-30, Marshal of the Soviet Union G.F. Odintsov noted: 'There will never be anything better than this howitzer.'

In many respects, the D-1 howitzer resembled the M-30. Its power, however, was substantially greater because of the high calibre of its shells.

The Soviet BM-21 'Grad' rocket launchers did, in fact, determine the outcome of the battle for Damansky Island. Their appearance in the area of combat operations remained unnoticed by the Chinese, and their sudden use resulted in great losses in the ranks of the Chinese Army subunits.

A curious fact is that it was namely on 15 March 1969 that the 'Grad' was used for the first time under combat conditions. Having found out about this and having analysed the results, several Western experts concluded that the Soviets had a new miracle weapon.

The M-240 mortar (240mm) attempted to destroy the Leonov tank. This system was adopted into the weapon inventory in 1950, although the development of the mortar was ongoing during the Great Patriotic War, and several models had even appeared under combat conditions. The shell for the M-240 weighed around 140 kilograms; therefore, it took as many as six soldiers to load the mortar.

Practically speaking, aviation was not used during

guns, which appeared on the Chinese riverbank at the height of the second engagement (about 3.5 kilometres from Damansky). Soviet howitzer artillery, however, almost immediately covered the self-propelled gun positions: one blew up, a second burned, and the remaining two vehicles hid in the forest. Thus, infantry, supported by mortars and artillery, played the main role in the fighting against the Chinese on the border.

The Soviets also used artillery – the 122mm M-30 howitzer, the 152mm D-1 howitzer and the 130mm M-46 cannon. It was the M-30 that on 15 March struck the Chinese positions simultaneously with the 'Grad' gun. As for the D-1 and the M-46, these guns conducted fire on 17 March during an unsuccessful attempt by a Soviet evacuation subunit to pull a damaged T-62 tank from the battlefield.

The M-30 had already been introduced into the Red Army inventory in 1938. However, its exceptional combat and exploitation qualities ensured decades of unfailing service for this weapon.

the border conflict, with the exception of the Mi-4 helicopters which the Soviets used to evacuate the wounded from the battlefield.

Although the fighting of 1969 had a local character and lasted for a relatively short period of time, the lessons were taken seriously. For example, the question arose concerning the development of a light and mobile weapon for motorised rifle subunits that would make it possible to inflict instantaneous losses on large masses of enemy infantry (the so-called 'human waves' used by the Chinese on Damansky). The Soviet AGS-17 automatic grenade launcher became such a weapon.

Chinese military specialists also drew some conclusions from the Damansky events. The results of using the 'Grad' made the greatest impression on them. It is, therefore, not surprising that some time later the PRC began work on developing analogous systems. This work continued for several years and was completed at the beginning of the 1980s with the adoption into their Army of salvo

Positions of Soviet M-30 howitzers in the Damansky area, March 1969. (Military Museum of Hanoi, via Albert Grandolini)

fire rocket systems, comparable to the 'Grad' with respect to their characteristics.

And the last thing worth mentioning. There is still no reliable information on how good the weapons produced in China were during the fighting on the border. On the other hand, it is known that the Soviet weapons demonstrated exceptional reliability and high combat qualities. There was not a single instance where weapons did not operate faultlessly, not a single instance of equipment breaking down as a result of some defect in design. And it is true when they say: say what you will, but the Soviet Union always knew how to make weapons.

8

HOW IT ALL ENDED

The discussion in the Kremlin of the battles on the border showed that Soviet leaders had different points of view on the prospects for the further development of events. The military, headed by Minister of Defence Marshal A.A. Grechko, proposed to deliver a preventive strike against Chinese nuclear facilities. At first glance, such a radical idea could be explained by the military's inherent decisiveness and inclination toward the use of force. Upon careful consideration, however, Grechko's proposal does not seem so reckless: in fact, he proposed a demonstration of force for the Chinese in order to force them to reject exacerbating tensions on the border. And, after all, this was the result, inasmuch as Peking stopped the provocations only after they had been decisively repelled along the entire length of the Sino-Soviet border.

At the end of August 1969, Mao Zedong found out about talks between Soviet leaders and leaders of other socialist countries. The theme of the talks was the attitude of the USSR's allies towards a strike against Chinese nuclear facilities.

At present, it is known that the US, and possibly other major world powers, were also making similar inquiries. Thus, on 18 August 1969, a very unusual conversation between B.N. Davydov, second secretary of the Soviet embassy, and one of the US State Department's staff members took place during lunch at the restaurant in the Americana Hotel.[1] Davydov began the conversation with some secondary questions about Vietnam, but quickly switched to the China theme. Without resorting to any verbal manoeuvring, the Soviet diplomat asked what the reaction of the American leadership would be to a preventive strike by the USSR against Chinese nuclear facilities. Struck by this news, the American made it clear how

serious this conversation was. Davydov confirmed the seriousness of the conversation, and then explained the goals that the USSR was pursuing in planning such an operation. First, the Chinese nuclear threat would be eliminated for decades. Second, such a strike would weaken and discredit Mao and his group to such an extent, that the army commanders and party cadre who did not agree with him would be able to seize power in Peking.

Of course, the American official could not give an immediate direct response to this question. He did, however, think it was possible to predict the initial US reaction to a possible aggravation of relations between the USSR and China. In his words, the administration of the United States would be following very attentively the course of events and would try not to become a participant in the conflict. Naturally he asked: What goal were the Soviet leaders pursuing in having these consultations with the US?

Most probably there are two versions. The first is that in Moscow the Kremlin was actually working out a variant of a surprise strike against Chinese nuclear facilities and, therefore, needed information on possible reactions by interested countries. Also completely probable, however, is that Moscow did not plan to attack China, but only wanted to prepare the ground for talks with Peking. If this was so, then it was counting on an information leak: in fact, the Soviet leaders wanted Peking to find out about the consultations and make serious conclusions about this.

On 10 September 1969, US Secretary of State William Rogers presented a memorandum to President Richard Nixon, which analysed the possibility of a Soviet strike against China.[2] The main conclusion was that this development of events was possible, but not very probable. Thus, everything hung on the skill of the politicians.

Aleksey Nikolayevich Kosygin, Chairman of the USSR Council of Ministers, belonged to that segment of the Soviet leadership that thought it was possible to settle the border problem peacefully. Yu.V. Andropov, Chairman of the KGB, also held this opinion. L.I. Brezhnev always reckoned with Kosygin's and Andropov's opinion, and, therefore, the advocates of the peaceful variant won this time.

On 21 March 1969, Kosygin tried to telephone Mao or Zhou Enlai. The special communications operator, however, refused to connect him with the Chinese leadership; allegedly, the refusal was expressed in the sense that there was no reason for the PRC leaders to speak with the 'Soviet revisionists.' Many researchers have written about this episode, but none of them focused on one obvious circumstance: no operator could independently make such decisions. It is clear that he was only obeying a direct order from one of China's leaders.

Attempts to establish direct contacts through diplomatic channels also were not crowned with success. Subsequently, the Soviets several times made persistent efforts to arrange a dialogue with Peking; time and again, however, they were met with the lack of desire on the part of the Chinese to engage in talks.

On 6 September, a delegation headed by Kosygin arrived in Hanoi to take part in the funeral events upon the death of Ho Chi Minh, the leader of Vietnam. Inasmuch as a Chinese delegation, headed by Li Xiangnian, was there, the Soviet prime minister decided to use that opportunity to arrange contacts. Vietnamese diplomats acted as mediators in this matter. Li Xiangnian received a communication about Kosygin's wish to stop in Peking after the funeral and discuss with the Chinese leaders the situation that had developed. Practically immediately a corresponding dispatch was sent to Mao Zedong and Zhou Enlai.

After thinking over the proposal, Mao agreed. That being said, however, there was one condition: the meeting was to be informal and take place outside of the Chinese capital. Peking Airport was deemed to be the best place. Then, a glitch occurred which almost spoiled the entire affair: the Chinese embassy in Hanoi received Peking's answer on the morning of 10 October, but Kosygin had already flown off to Moscow, across India.

Feeling responsible for the possible thwarting of the talks because of a stupid technical problem, the Chinese leaders persevered. Firstly, they let the Soviet ambassador in Vietnam know – again, by the way, via Vietnamese diplomats – that they had agreed to the talks. Secondly, they informed A.I. Yelizavetin, interim USSR Consul General in China, that Zhou Enlai had agreed to meet at Peking Airport. Guided by the interests of the matter, Kosygin quickly flew to Peking from Tashkent (where he was at that moment).

On 11 September 1969, talks between A.N. Kosygin and Zhou Enlai took place at the Peking Airport. Other Soviets in attendance were Secretary of the CC CPSU K.F. Katushev and Deputy Chairman of the Supreme Soviet M.A. Yasnov; other Chinese in attendance were Deputy Premiers of the PRC State Council Li Xiangnian and Xie Fuzhi. The meeting last three and one-half hours.

During the talks, Kosygin particularly stressed the need for the quickest resolution of all differences that had accumulated between the two countries. Zhou Enlai did not object, but his main priority was the resolution of the border issues. He declared that 'China has no territorial claims with regard to the Soviet Union' and acknowledged the current border.[3] At the same time, he raised the issue of the so-called 'disputed sectors,' that is, those territories that at one time belonged to China, but were then seized as a result of the

so-called 'unequal treaties.' However, the Soviet delegation declined to discuss this issue phrased in this way, because if they did, an impression could have been made that Kosygin and his colleagues were acknowledging the defects of treaties concerning the border that were in force at that time, thereby creating a foundation for further discussion of this problem from an angle that the Chinese needed. Therefore, the head of the Soviet government limited himself only to the observation that the work of experts was needed here. The main result of the discussion was an agreement that hostile actions on the Sino-Soviet border would cease and that troops would halt on those lines they were occupying when the talks began.

It must be mentioned that Zhou Enlai proposed the phrase 'the sides stay where they are at this time,' but Kosygin immediately agreed to it. It was namely at that moment that Damansky Island and Kirkinsky Island became *de facto* Chinese!

To understand this unexpected conclusion, one must attentively follow the development of events in the area of the island after the March battles ended.

And so, Chinese troops had been driven out of Soviet territory. The Damansky area was transferred to the 135th Division. A month and a half later, when the situation had stabilised, the island retuned once again to the border guards. They did not, however, go on Damansky Island, but rather set up fire cover. Any attempt by the Chinese to set foot on the island was interdicted by sniper and machine-gun fire.

On 10 September 1969, the border guards received an order to cease fire. Immediately after this, the Chinese came to the island and established themselves there. The same occurred on Kirkinsky Island on that very same day.

Thus, on 11 September, the day of the Peking talks, the Chinese were on Damansky Island and Kirkinsky Island. That meant that Kosygin's agreement to the wording, 'the sides stay where they are at this time,' was, in fact, the surrender of the islands to China. With regard to this, at least two questions rise:

1. Did the Soviet leader know of the Chinese presence on the islands on the day of the talks?
2. If he knew, then why did he agree to Zhou Enlai's proposal?

The answer to the first question is: he knew. The 10 September order to cease fire was issued only to create a favourable climate for the commencement of the talks. The Soviet leaders knew well that the Chinese had settled on the islands and willingly accepted this.

The answer to the second question is: the Kremlin decided that sooner or later a new border would have to be drawn along the channels of the Amur and Ussuri Rivers. There was no reason to hold on to these scraps of land, since they were going to be handed over to the Chinese anyway.

The islands on the Amur and Ussuri, as well as sectors of the border territory in Kazakhstan, had not been conquered by the Chinese. Just the opposite: the PLA had been defeated on the battlefield. The Soviet leadership simply handed over all this land to the Chinese; for the Soviets, the main thing under these conditions was to establish peace and stability on the border.

Soon after the talks ended, Kosygin and Zhou exchanged letters, in which they agreed to begin work on a nonaggression treaty. The Soviet and Chinese border guards received from the appropriate authorities of their states the following instructions:

1. To maintain normal relations with their neighbours and uphold the existing borderline.

Soviet border guards observe the Chinese side. Damansky region, 8 April 1969. (Military Museum of Hanoi, via Albert Grandolini)

Chinese soldiers on Damansky after the battles had ended. (Chinese internet)

2. To resolve all border issues peacefully and in a friendly manner, without threats or the use of force.

3. To take into consideration the interests of the civilians of the neighbouring side in the sphere of economic activities.

4. Not to conduct any propaganda against their neighbours (including use of loudspeakers).

On 19 October 1969, a government delegation from the USSR, headed by First Deputy Minister of Foreign Affairs V.V. Kuznetsov, arrived in Peking for talks on border issues. The Chinese delegation for the talks was headed by Deputy Minister of Foreign Affairs

Qiao Guanhua. Judging by everything, at that time these were the most experienced diplomats from the two countries: Kuznetsov had been viewed for a long time as a candidate for the post of minister, and Qiao Guanhua subsequently was minister of foreign affairs for more than two years.

Unfortunately, the nascent relaxation of tensions did not develop, and the blame here lay completely on the Chinese.

The fact is that in the Peking leadership, Minister of Defence Lin Biao's group, who saw Moscow's treachery in everything, held the strongest position. It was in just this way that they interpreted Kosygin's position at the talks with Zhou. As for Mao, he considered the Soviet peace initiatives as only a screen for the preparation of a strike against China. As proof, he cited intelligence about the readiness of Soviet strategic forces and the fact that no one from the higher Soviet leadership had met Kosygin at the Moscow airport (thereby, in Mao's opinion, expressing their attitude toward the results of the talks).

Zhou Enlai may have thought otherwise, but his many years as part of China's leadership was conditioned by a peculiar division of labour: Mao handled politics and Zhou handled the economy. Zhou may have been a principled man, only not with regard to Mao. For Zhou Enlai, Mao Zedong was 'God, and emperor, and military chief.' Thus, for the premier, Mao's words were always decisive, even when Zhou intrinsically did not agree with the 'great helmsman.' It appears that the war on the border with the USSR was just such a case.

Many Soviet/Russia sources who met personally with Zhou Enlai recall this man with unwavering sympathy. Some go farther, saying that Premier Zhou would never have allowed a worsening of relations with the USSR, but he did not have enough power.

Recently, however, works have appeared whose authors question Zhou's friendly attitude toward the Soviet Union.[4] Instead, they name Marshal Lin Biao as the real advocate of Chinese friendship with its northern neighbour. As for Mao, they say that, in general, he had arranged things well for himself, having two main assistants – the 'good' Premier Zhou Enlai and the 'evil' supervisor of special services Kang Sheng.

Apparently, each of the sides in this dispute has its own arguments and counterarguments. From the position of the ordinary Soviet citizens, they were all 'good' – Mao and Zhou and Lin, and other PRC leaders. They all had a hand in the deification of Mao Zedong, the unleashing of the 'cultural revolution,' and the escalation of hostility between the Chinese and the Soviet people. From this point of view, attempts to divide Mao's supporters into 'good' and 'evil' seem like too abstract an exercise, having little in common with real life.

So what happened after the meeting at Peking Airport?

A new cycle of military psychosis in Peking did not contribute to normalising relations with the USSR, although the fighting on the border did end.

Then, the border talks began, alternating between Moscow and Peking. Having, in fact, given Damansky and Kirkinsky to the Chinese, the Soviets from time to time protested and demanded that the Chinese leave the islands. For example, such protests were made at different levels on 3 November 1969, 30 December 1969, 12 and 13 February 1970, and 1 April 1970. It is difficult to say what the Kremlin was counting on here, but each Soviet dispatch caused another outburst of emotion. The Soviets who took part in the talks accused the Chinese of violating agreements, of sneaking onto the islands, etc. The latter were outraged at such a treatment of events, inasmuch as the Chinese border guards went to Damansky and Kirkinsky openly, as soon as the firing against them from the Soviet riverbank stopped.

The talks were often reminiscent of a conversation between two deaf people, so much did they not understand one another. The following is a characteristic example that demonstrates the overall situation at the talks:

V.V. Kuznetsov: "Taking advantage of the fact that after 11 September 1969 the Soviets undertook specific measures with regard to creating a normal situation on the border, the Chinese stealthily, sometimes at night, began to go to sectors and took measures there that the Soviet Union could not ignore and could not let pass: i.e., you violated the existing border. .."

Qiao Guanhua: "To which of these islands did we go stealthily at night after 11 September 1969?"

V. V. Kuznetsov: ".. . You came to these islands without any consultation."

Qiao Guanhua: ".. . Your posing of the question this way may pique us: after all, you used the word 'stealthily.' Where is this 'stealthily'?"

Chai Chengwen: ".. . You have not answered which sectors we came to in secret, at night. If you do not answer, then this is slander."

Qiao Guanhua: "This statement is a threat and insult to China as a great power. Your note is false from beginning to end."

V.V. Kuznetsov answered that it was the Chinese note that was false.[5]

Further discussions continued in the same spirit – with mutual accusations, insults, and an absolute lack of understanding of one another. Naturally, all Soviet protests turned out to be only a waste of breath: the Chinese never did leave the islands. In general, this minor episode shows how inconsistent Moscow's position was at the talks in Peking.

Chinese sources also provide their own description of the talks in Peking; the affair is presented as if all initiatives had come from the Chinese delegation, while the Soviet representatives only listened and gave in. For example, the

following can be read on the official site of the PRC Ministry of Foreign Affairs:

In order to reduce the tension of military confrontation between China and the Soviet Union, at the request of the Soviets Premier Zhou Enlai met with Chairman of the USSR Council of Ministers A.N. Kosygin at Peking Airport on 11 September 1969 and discussed with him the urgent issues of Sino-Soviet relations, especially the border question. Premier Zhou Enlai said: "Chairman Mao Zedong told you about five years ago that our discussions about differences in theoretical issues could continue for ten thousand years. These discussions were limited to theoretical issues on which you can have your own point of view and we ours. They should not affect relations between the two countries. In today's world, polemics because of differences of opinions is completely natural. Even when communism will prevail, or even in ten thousand years, disagreements and disputes will still remain."

Later, Premier Zhou Enlai focused Chairman Kosygin's attention on the following: "As for the border conflicts, China has always been on the defensive. One look at the map is enough to see: all of this year's border conflicts have occurred in disputed sectors. You always claim that we want to fight, but why should we want to, when we have so many domestic problems? We have a huge country that needs to be developed. We have no troops on foreign territory, and we do not intend to invade any foreign country. You, however, have sent a large number of troops to the Far East. You claim that you want to wage a nuclear war, knowing well the current capabilities of our nuclear weapons." Later, Premier Zhou emphasised: "Discussions should be conducted without the use of force. You said that you will destroy of our nuclear bases with a preventive strike. In that case, we will declare that this is war and aggression. We will decisively fight against this and will fight to the end."

Psychosis in China: local inhabitants dig shelters in the courtyards of their homes. (Chinese Internet)

Premier Zhou also claimed that discussions between China and the Soviet Union on the issue of principles should not hinder the normalisation of state relations; that the two countries must not fight each other because of the border issue; that the Sino-Soviet talks about the border should be conducted without the use of threats. Chairman Kosygin agreed with all this. Regarding a proposal from the Chinese, mutual understanding was achieved on the following points: first and foremost, to sign an agreement on measures for maintaining the *status quo* on the border, preventing armed conflicts, and disengaging the armed forces on both sides of the border in the disputed sectors, and then to conduct talks on resolving the border issue. This meeting resulted in a resumption of Sino-Soviet talks in October 1969 in Peking.[6]

Calling attention to itself is the fact that the above-cited text has no date, and, therefore, it is not known if it was taken from old sources or written recently. The author is also unknown.

If we talk about the essence of the cited text, then Zhou Enlai, deliberately or inadvertently, clearly identified the reason that the conflict arose: in fact, the Chinese leadership did not want a major war against the USSR, inasmuch as 'we have so many domestic problems.' It was namely for the sake of resolving their domestic problems that Mao and his entourage organised the bloodshed on the border, that is, they were trying to absolve themselves from all the mistakes of the 'cultural revolution' and shift the blame for the catastrophic consequences of their policies onto the Soviet Union.

9
WHAT NEXT?

On 16 May 1991, the *Agreement between the Union of Soviet Socialist Republics and the People's Republic of China on the Eastern Part of the Sino-Soviet State Border* was signed in Moscow, in accordance with which the border on the rivers ran along the main channel or along the middle, depending on whether or not the river was navigable. The text also contained an agreement about setting up a demarcation committee.

On 13 February 1992, no longer the Soviet, but the Russian Supreme Council ratified this agreement, with R.I. Khasbulatov, chairman of the Presidium of the Supreme Council of Russia, and Speaker of the State Council, signing the corresponding document. The Chinese completed this procedure on 25 February 1992, and on 16 March the instruments of ratification were exchanged in Peking. Thus, the Agreement went into effect on 16 March 1992, in accordance with which the border boundaries extending around 4,150 kilometres – from Mongolia to North Korea – were specified.

On 3 September 1994, another agreement was signed in Moscow, this one concerning the western part of the Sino-Soviet state border. The issue in this agreement was the border sector extending around 50 kilometres in the Altay Mountains. The agreement went into effect on 17 October 1995.

Talks on the demarcation of the border between the USSR and China resulted in the fact that many islands on border rivers were given to the PRC, including Damansky, now under its new name –Zhenbaodao – meaning 'treasure island.' The island acquired its name – so unexpected and so familiar for all readers of adventures – because of its outline bearing a striking similarity to an ancient Chinese coin, the *yuanbao*, a symbol of happiness and wealth. The former Kirkinsky Island also acquired a new name, Qiliqin.

Kamennaya Hill, in the Lake Zhalanashkol region, also became Chinese. A monument commemorating the events of a half-century ago was placed at the foot of the hill.

The agreements that were signed did not resolve all the border issues. After the agreements were concluded, there were still some disputed territories in the Khabarovsk area (Bolshoy Ussuriysky Island and Tarabarov Island) and Bolshoy Island on the Argun River.

In 2004, Russian President Putin visited Peking, at which time an agreement regarding the disputed territories was achieved: Tarabarov Island and the western part of Bolshoy Ussuriysky Island were given to China, Bolshoy Island was divided approximately in half between Russia and the PRC. In 2005, after the completion of all judicial procedures, the border was demarked – this, in fact, ended the history of the border delineation between the two countries. Now, only displays in some Russian and Chinese museums, and the rows of tombstones in military cemeteries serve as a reminder of these events.

The reaction of the Russian people to handing over territory to China was basically negative. Of course, it is natural to think that it is much better to receive than to give. As for the politicians, diplomats, and scholars, their opinions diverged. Some said that the decision that had been made made it possible to eliminate the potential threat of a new conflict on the border; others pointed out the possibility of other neighbours of the Russian Federation boosting their claims to Russian territory. In China, the agreements that had been achieved were perceived with pride, inasmuch as the acquisition of land attested that the country had a strong position and its interests were being taken into consideration: the weak never obtained anything.

All this – the emotions of the ordinary citizen, the arguments 'for' and 'against' the new border between Russia and China – can be understood. Now, however, another question must be answered: did the territorial dispute between two countries end this way, or is a recurrence possible, from the perspective of returning to the situation at the end of the 1960s?

Formally, everything seems to be in order, and officials display complete satisfaction with the agreements that were concluded. There are, however, warning signals. For example, in China it is still not considered shameful to exaggerate concerns over the theme of any 'injustices' regarding a new Sino-Soviet borderline, whether this takes place on the level of Internet discussions or somewhere in the local press. However, inasmuch as in the PRC the ideological sphere is under the strict control of the authorities, one can conclude that these very authorities are favourably inclined to this kind of discussion. The following is an example of how scholars from the PRC Academy of Social Sciences see the future development of events:[1]

Under conditions where the material resources of the Far East, including the resources of Siberia and Central Asia, are linked with the finances and technical resources of Japan and the western coast of the Pacific Ocean (the "four small dragons"), and also

Zhenbao (formerly Damansky) today. The photo was taken from the Chinese riverbank of the Ussuri River approximately at the place where the Chinese command post was located during the March 1969 fighting. (Chinese Internet)

Kamennaya Hill: today it is PRC territory. (Chinese Internet)

with the enormous human resources of China, and where they find some form of integration, this will result in the appearance of an extremely vast area on the Earth's surface, where the most powerful centre in history of a new industrial civilisation will be formed.[2]

To translate this into simple language, this means: money – Japanese and those with them; population – Chinese; and land – Russian (Siberia and the Far East).

The following is another excerpt from the work of Chinese social scientists:

From the moment private property and state resources appeared, which originally belonged to all mankind, they were divided unevenly among various countries and regions, as a result of which countries and regions poor in resources were forced to constantly make up for the shortage of resources by means of trade and other methods, and then, in the process of material transformation, increase their added value and exchange what they received for an even greater amount of resources.[3]

From here, the conclusion suggests itself: the 'unequal' distribution of resources among countries is clearly unjust; therefore, something must be changed in favour of the deprived.

It should be mentioned here that not only Russian specialists, but also ordinary citizens who for some reason have contact with the Chinese notice such insinuations and poorly concealed plans. Here is a specific example.

The recollections of border guard V.M. Tirskikh, who served in the Iman Border Detachment, have already been cited. After his service in the border guards, Viktor Mikhaylovich completed flight school and became a pilot. Recently he has been involved with freight transportation. He wrote the following:

Visiting China quite often because of service obligations, I never cease to be surprised at how fast its economy is developing. I saw

The Dalnerechensk cemetery. Tombstones of the border guards and Soviet Army soldiers who died on Damansky Island. (from Ivan, a reader of books about Damansky)

Hutou across the river in 1968. It seemed as if poverty would never leave China. At the airport in Tianjin I looked at the map hanging in their control room and asked a Chinese customer (they speak Russian): "Why does Northern Kashmir, a territory of India, have the same colour as China?" The answer came from a 27–30-year-old man: "But this is our territory. And this, and that." His hand swept over the entire Primorsky Province and moved along Siberia and Kazakhstan.[4]

These days, Chinese stores sell maps on which vast areas of Siberia and the Far East are noted as former Chinese territories (see colour section for map).

The description of past events in history textbooks is given under headings such as 'Russia's Seizure of a Considerable Part of Our Country,' 'Russia's Seizure of Territory in Northern China,' etc. As events in 1969 demonstrated, it is very easy, if necessary, to transform such information into a feeling of revenge and an attempt to restore justice that has been trampled on.

Another example demonstrates what such a treatment of history leads to. In the 2 July 2020 edition of the *South China Morning Post*, one of Hong Kong's oldest English-language newspapers, an article by Eduardo Baptista, 'Why Russia's Vladivostok Celebration Prompted a Nationalist Backlash in China,' was published. The article told about the reaction of Chinese users of the Weibo social network to the celebration in Russia of the 160th anniversary of the founding of Vladivostok. The following is an excerpt from this article:

When the Russian embassy posted a video on Weibo of a party held on Thursday to celebrate the 160th anniversary of the founding of the city, whose name means "ruler of the east" in Russian, it prompted an online backlash.

Shen Shiwei, a journalist for the state-owned broadcaster CGTN, tweeted that the post "recalled people's memories [of] those humiliated days in 1860s."

Zhang Heqing, a Chinese diplomat working in the embassy in Pakistan, commented "isn't this what in the past was our Haishenwai?," referring to the Chinese name for the area before its annexation.

Meanwhile, one Weibo user posted: "Today we can only endure, but the Chinese people will remember, and one generation after another will continue to remember!" and another wrote "We must believe that this ancestral land will return home in the future!"[5]

Two points deserve attention here:

1. The Chinese diplomat thinks, with perfect candour, that it is completely possible to question that Vladivostok belongs to Russia – and keep in mind that, as a rule, diplomats are very careful about what they say. This means that Zhang Heqing knew for sure that there would be no censure from the higher leadership. Perhaps they would even praise him?

2. These responses show that there are enough people in China who are ready to quickly present territorial claims to Russia. They are only waiting for an order 'from above.'

Whatever Russian diplomats might say today, settling the border issue with China meant handing over part of Russian territory to the

PRC. And those who declare that signed documents are perpetual either do not understand the logic of historical development or are consciously engaging in wishful thinking. After all, even basic everyday experience teaches that there is nothing perpetual in our world, and any treaty only records the balance of forces of the sides at a given moment. With time, however, the balance may change, and then those who have the advantage will clearly be able to pose the question of a change in agreements that had been concluded earlier.

There is no doubt that Russia's higher leadership understands this well. Apparently, it is namely this understanding that also conditioned all Sino-Soviet global projects, such as the 'Power of Siberia' gas pipeline. After all, stable delivery of energy over the safest route objectively stimulates the Chinese leadership to appreciate and safeguard a calm situation on the Sino-Soviet border. This, of course, does not mean that this calm is absolutely guaranteed and that problems in the future are not foreseen. Therefore, for the Russian leadership the ability to defend its territory is a problem that cannot be resolved overnight: it will always be on the agenda.

Recently, events have occurred in the world that have pushed Russia and China into close cooperation with each other. Sensing a weakening of American influence in the world, US leaders are trying to play on existing disagreements among various states so as to weaken competitors and prolong their dominance in this way. Up to now, however, Russia and China have managed to successfully manoeuvre and not allow the Americans to drive a wedge between them. Russia sees China as a rich customer for traditional Russian export goods and a supplier of products that it cannot buy in the West because of sanctions that have been imposed. China, in turn, is extremely interested in Russian energy carriers and military technologies.

It is possible that China is also counting on Russia's help in case of a direct military conflict with the US. That being said, however, one should not forget that while national states and borders between them exist, interests, and not emotions, will set the tone. Now,

under conditions of a trade war with the US, China is suddenly talking about the fact that the economic systems of Russia and the PRC mutually supplement one another, and, therefore, they say cooperation must be strengthened. However, not too long ago China abstained from voting in the UN Security Council, when Russia needed support more than ever, but Chinese banks, in fact, supported the American sanctions and refused to cooperate with Russian financial organisations. As they say, it is nothing personal – it is only business.

Let us return to the question posed in the title of this last chapter: 'What next?' The authors could follow the example of many political scientists and experts and speculate about the possible development of events around the Sino-Russian border. However, we will not bore the reader, inasmuch as our account of the Sino-Soviet border war of 1969 is practically finished. Frankly, we admit that we do not know the answer to this question. And, by the way, the above-mentioned political scientists and experts do not know the answer either. The contemporary world has become so complex, and so many varied problems and challenges have arisen, that we can hardly give a reliable forecast, even for tomorrow, that would tell us about long-term prospects. There is, however, a feeling that the tensions in international relations that clearly exist now are the result of changes in the balance of power of the principal players that are occurring in the world arena. In precisely this way the events on the Sino-Soviet border in their time posed the question of a new balance of power on the threshold of the 1970s. After all, having challenged the powerful Soviet Union, China declared its interests and claims to the whole world, its attitude toward which had become completely different than before the fighting on the border. We hope that the current generation of world leaders is responsible enough and self-controlled enough so that a new balance will be achieved without gunfire and without victims.

APPENDIX I

ANNOUNCEMENT BY THE GOVERNMENT OF THE USSR

On 29 March of this year, the government of the USSR addressed the government of the PRC with a proposal to immediately take practical measures to normalise the situation on the Sino-Soviet border. In its announcement the USSR called upon the government of the PRC to refrain from actions on the border that could cause complications, such as took place in the area of Damansky Island, and to resolve differences, if they arise, calmly and through talks.

The Soviet Government proposed to renew consultations for the purpose of determining precisely where the border line runs on individual border sectors; these consultations began in 1964 in Peking and were discontinued by the Chinese. The Soviets suggested 15 April as a possible date for the first meeting between representatives of the USSR and the PRC, or 'another time in the near future that is convenient for the Chinese.'

On 24 May of this year, the government of the People's Republic of China gave its answer. From this, it follows that the government of the PRC agrees with the proposal to conduct talks, announces its readiness to agree upon a time and place to begin them through diplomatic channels, and speaks out against the employment of military force.

Thus, it would seem that the path to the negotiation table has been opened.

The current tension between the Soviet Union and the PRC was caused exclusively by actions on the part of the Chinese. If the Chinese government also proceeds from the necessity of maintaining normal relations between the USSR and the PRC, acknowledging the principle of non-interference in each other's internal affairs and respecting territorial integrity and inviolability, then the situation on the border will once again become normal. Such a development of events would meet the fundamental interests of the Soviet people and, we are sure, the interests of the Chinese people as well.

In the opinion of the Soviet Government, the fact that an announcement by the PRC government put forward a number of claims and demands for the Soviet Union, for which there is not the slightest basis and which can have only one purpose – to add new complications to those that the Chinese created earlier – does not contribute to creating a favourable atmosphere for talks.

Apparently, the Chinese decided to assess some facts from the history of relations between Russia and China in the hopes that, through manipulation and deliberate distortions, a picture of how the borders between our two countries were arrived at would be created, which is desirable for the Chinese, but completely untrue.

That being said, the question about the so-called 'unequal treaties,' as the PRC government calls the treaties that defined the current border between the Soviet Union and the People's Republic of China, has once again advanced to the foreground. Under the contrived pretence of eliminating the 'inequalities' that were allowed in past centuries, the Chinese government is attempting to justify claims to half a million square kilometres of indigenous Soviet territory.

The Chinese government did not want to make the subject of the discussions between the USSR and the PRC the clarification of the line passing through the border, which was the topic of the 1964 consultations, but rather wanted to discuss the issue of a new Sino-Soviet border from the standpoint of how the Chinese now interpret history and the treaties.

One cannot help but focus attention on the fact that territorial claims against other states occupy a very large place in China's current foreign policy and propaganda. Chinese leaders today claim land which Chinese conquerors entered or intended to enter sometime in the past.

This kind of propaganda did not begin today or yesterday. It has been spread subtly – from the glorification of the aggressive policies of the feudal lords of the past, from the publication after 1949 of textbooks and maps in which numerous lands of other states were depicted as Chinese land. Then the territorial claims began to be officially advanced.

Since the 1960s their expansionist ambitions have been openly turned toward the Soviet Union as well. Arbitrarily manipulating historical information or the lack thereof, the Chinese are attempting, no matter what the cost, to create a so-called territorial question between the USSR and the PRC, and to cast doubt on the existing borderline between them. This circumstance has stimulated us to illuminate the facts of this question.

The 29 March Announcement of the Soviet Government already noted that the Sino-Soviet border is the result of long historical development. When relations between the Russian state and China were first established, a vast, sparsely populated or practically unpopulated, semi-desert taiga lay between them. At this time, for example, the northern state border of China was identified as the Great Wall of China, which ran for around 4,000 kilometres and which, as is known, is located more than one thousand kilometres southwest of the Amur and Ussuri Rivers.

At the time Russian settlers claimed the Amur region in the first half of the XVII century, Manchuria was a state that was independent of China, and had been settled by people who were ethnically completely different from the Chinese (the Hans). Moreover, it was namely during this time that the Chinese themselves had lost independence and had become a part of the Manchurian state, after the Manchurians captured Peking (1644) and imposed the domination of the Qing Dynasty upon the Chinese people. Right up until the end of the XIX century, Manchuria, in fact, remained a separate entity – a specific possession of the emperors, where Chinese were forbidden to settle or engage in business activities.

At the end of the XVII century, Manchurian Emperor Kangxi organised a number of military campaigns against the Russian settlements of the Albazin Voivodeship on the Amur River. In this regard, a report from Manchurian commanders to their emperor noted: '… the lands lying to the northeast for several thousand li,[1] which never before belonged to China, have become part of our domain.' For some time these lands were held by the Manchurian invaders.

At the end of the XVII–beginning of the XVIII centuries, the Manchurian rulers conquered Mongolia and destroyed the Dzhungar Khanate of the Oirats, killing more than a million people – a large portion of its population – and subjugated the Uyghur state in Eastern Turkestan (Kashgaria).[2] In this way, vast areas, up to now called Xinjiang (meaning 'new border'), populated by Uyghurs, Kazakhs, Kirgiz, Dhungans, and other nationalities, fell under the authority of the Qing emperors. At the same time, Manchurian–Chinese expansion moved in southwestern and southern directions.

This is how the activities look if we keep to the actual facts and do not treat them arbitrarily. Qing China in no way was only an object of some foreign aggression. The Manchurian–Chinese emperors were bogdykhans,[3] who lived off the Chinese people and actively carried out a predatory colonial policy, adding to their domains piece after piece of land from other countries and other peoples. The process of the formation of Chinese territory in the current borders was accompanied by the coercive assimilation of oppressed nationalities and their physical annihilation. Today's historiographers, however, are only looking for 'arguments' in the actions of the bogdykhans and mandarins to justify expansionist intentions.

The border between the Soviet Union and China, which was formed many generations ago, reflected and reflects the actual settlement of lands by the peoples of these two states along the natural mountain and river lines. This border was formed legally, specifically, and clearly over its entire extent by treaties, protocols, and maps.

The Treaty of Aigun, which formed the border along the Amur River, was signed on 16 May 1858 in the town of Aigun by Governor General N. Muravyev as the representative of the Russian state, and Heilongjiang Commander-in-Chief Yi Shan as the representative of the Daiqing ('Great Qing') state. As its preamble stated, this treaty was concluded 'by common agreement, for the sake of the greater eternal mutual friendship between the two states, for the benefit of their subjects … ' The treaty was approved by a decree by the bogdykhan on 2 June 1958, and ratified by Russia on 8 July 1858.

The Treaty of Tianjin was signed on 1 July 1858 in the town of Tianjin by Putyatin, Russia's imperial commissar in China, and Hua Shan, a high dignitary representing China. The treaty foresaw that portions of the border between Russia and China that had not been specified would be immediately studied on the spot by trusted persons from both governments, 'who will agree on the boundary line.' The Treaty of Tianjin went on to say 'Upon the designation of the border, a detailed description and maps of the adjoining area will be made, which will also serve in the future as incontestable documents about the borders for both governments.'

To implement this agreement, a treaty was concluded in Peking on 2 November 1860, which confirmed the agreements in Aigun and Tianjin that had been achieved earlier, and also determined the border along the Ussuri River. The Treaty of Peking was signed by N. Ignatyev as the representative of the Russian state, and 'Prince Gong, called Yi Xing' as the representative of the Daiqing state. In the Treaty of Peking both sides confirmed that it had been concluded ' … for the greater strengthening of the mutual friendship between the two empires, for the development of trade relations, and to prevent misunderstandings … ' A protocol was added as a component to this treaty in 1861 on the exchange of maps and descriptions of the demarcations in the Ussuri *Krai*.

All the above-mentioned documents, as well as other documents that determined the borders between the Soviet Union and China, remain valid interstate documents between the two countries to this day. Since this cannot be denied, the Chinese are trying to sow doubt as to the legitimacy of these legal acts, allowing outright falsification.

An announcement by the PRC government argues that the map attached to the 1860 Treaty of Peking, which shows how the borderline runs, was 'compiled unilaterally by tsarist Russia.' This is an outright lie. In fact, the protocol on exchanging maps was signed on 16 July 1861, on the one hand, by P. Kozakevich and K. Budogossky as commissars representing the Russian state, and,

on the other hand, by Cheng Qi and Jing Chun as commissars representing the Daiqing state. It was sealed in the name of Russia and China by official stamps.

The protocol said that 'after a final verification of all copies of the maps and descriptions …' and namely 'two maps of the borderline in Russian and Manchurian, which comprise the addendum to the Treaty of Peking … [and] likewise, four maps and descriptions of the border from the Ussuri to the sea … they were found to be in perfect agreement.' Further on the protocol notes that 'the first commissar of the Russian state handed over to the first commissar of the Daiqing state one copy of a detailed map of the border in Russian and Manchurian, and, having accepted the map, the first commissar of the Daiqing state, in turn, handed over to the Russian commissar the same map in the same languages. The other four maps with descriptions of the borders from the Ussuri to the sea were exchanged in the same way.' The stamps and signatures of the Russian and Chinese representatives were placed on all maps. The PRC government, however, despite the facts recorded in the documents, talks about some 'unilateral' compilation of the maps.

The announcement by the Chinese government states that Damansky Island 'has been Chinese territory from time immemorial,' and that the Ussuri River was 'an internal Chinese River' before 1860. However, historical facts also attest otherwise here. As was mentioned above, right up until the Manchurians conquered China, the northern borders of the Chinese state proper ran along the Great Wall of China, and had no contact at all with the Ussuri River. The Manchurians themselves at that time were living in the area of the Liaodong Peninsula and the Liaohe River, that is, a distance of 800 and more kilometres south and southwest of the Amur and Ussuri Rivers. At the end of the 1670s–beginning of the 1680s, the Manchurians identified the northern boundaries of their empire by the so-called 'Willow Palisade' – a line of fortifications and sentries that ran near Mukden. The state border guard patrolled this line, and if Manchurian subjects went beyond the external boundaries of the 'palisade,' this was viewed as going beyond the border, which is attested, in particular, by *Baqi Tongzhi Chuji* [The Description of the Eight Banners], a famous Chinese historical description of the armed forces of the Manchurian Empire. The remains of the 'Willow Palisade' can be seen even today. Thus, for the Manchurians the Ussuri could in no way have been and was not an 'internal river.'

The state demarcation in Primorye between tsarist Russia and the Manchurian–Chinese Qing Empire was completed in the second half of the XIX century. The 1860 Treaty of Peking specified the Ussuri River as the borderline between Russia and China; in accordance with a protocol attached to it in 1861, 'the borderline' on river sectors was indicated by a red line on the map. In the area of Damansky Island it ran directly along the Chinese riverbank and, consequently, this island, located on the Soviet side of the 'borderline,' belongs to the Soviet Union and not to China.

It is generally accepted that in international law there are no standards that automatically establish a border on border rivers along the middle of the river's main channel. In concluding the corresponding treaties, the states identified the border in a way that they considered it most appropriate, according to the circumstances. There are examples in relations between states where the border was established along a riverbank and not along a channel. The 1858 treaty between Costa Rica and Nicaragua established that the borderline ran along the right bank of the San Juan River, and 'the Republic of Nicaragua has the exclusive right of possession of and sovereign jurisdiction over the waters of this river.' Agreements between other countries have a similar determination of the border on rivers.

The 1860 Russian–Chinese Treaty of Peking is one of these examples. Acknowledgement that the borderline does not necessarily coincide with the channel was also reflected in the Sino-Soviet agreement on navigation procedures on border rivers, concluded in 1951. Article 1 of the agreement says that ships from both sides will sail along the main channel, 'regardless of where the state borderline runs.'

During the consultations in Peking in 1964, the Soviets expressed their readiness to meet the wishes of the Chinese, who were citing the interests of the Chinese coastal population, and to come to an agreement on the borderline between the USSR and the PRC along the Amur and Ussuri Rivers on the basis of mutual concessions, under the condition that the Chinese, in turn, express their readiness to correspondingly acknowledge the interests of the Soviet population on individual sectors of the border. This would have been a reasonable agreement, based on the two sides' attempt to remove the tension and maintain calm on the border.

At that time an agreement was not achieved, because the Chinese representatives complicated the consultations by advancing unjustified territorial and other demands, which put into question both the existing border line and all treaties that had specified the Sino-Soviet border.

An announcement by the PRC government, dated 24 May of this year, said that in contravention 'of the description of the state border between China and Russia in the Kashgar region' of 1884, the latter allegedly occupied more than 20,000 square kilometres of Chinese territory. Meanwhile, the 22 May 1884 protocol, to which the Chinese are referring, has no relation in general to the Pamir region, which anyone who takes the trouble to pick up this protocol will be convinced of. The Russian and Chinese commissars were occupied with where the border ran in the area of the Tian Shan Mountains between the former Russian Fergana Region and the Chinese Kashgar Region from the Bedel Pass to the Uz-Bel Pass, and upon completion of their work they signed the above-mentioned protocol, dated 22 May 1884. The demarcation in Pamir was done by an exchange of notes in 1894, when the sides agreed 'not to move beyond the positions which they now occupy' in Pamir and the Sarykol Range. This line, and no other, exists to this day.

In light of known facts, the arguments that China's border in the western sector 'runs along Lake Balkhash' look, at the very least, ridiculous. Russian fortifications and settlements were founded on the upper Irtysh River at the very beginning of the XVIII century. The Kazakh *zhuzy* (clans) in Northern and Eastern Kazakhstan had accepted Russian allegiance already in 1731 and 1740.

At this time the Manchurian Qing Empire was busy conquering Central Asia in the area of what is now Xinjiang, and suppressing resistance by the Oirats, Uyghurs, Kazakhs, and other nationalities who lived on the territory of Dzhungaria and Eastern Turkestan. The western border of the Qing invaders was separated from Lake Balkhash by several hundred kilometres.

After the capture of Dzhungaria in 1758, the Manchurians began to make sporadic plundering raids on the Kazakh and Kirgiz nomads. There were no military or civilian organs of authority of the Qing Empire whatsoever in Kazakhstan or in other areas of what is now the Soviet socialist republics of Central Asia, not to mention that there was never any civilian Manchurian or Chinese community here.

Thus, historical facts attest that the Chinese border in the west did not extend further than the provinces of Gansu and Sichuan, and, therefore, never reached Lake Balkhash.

II

In its announcement dated 29 March of this year, the Soviet Government already addressed the question of the attitude of the Soviet Union toward the unequal treaties, and attempts by the Chinese to disorient public opinion on this completely clear issue.

Immediately after the Great October Socialist Revolution, decrees by Lenin annulled all unequal and secret treaties that tsarist Russia had concluded with foreign states, including China. This step by the Soviet State expressed its determination to develop relations of friendship, equality, and mutual respect with all countries, including China.

A 25 July 1919 address by the government of the RSFSR to the Chinese people and to the governments of South and North China pointed out which specific treaties between Russia and China the Soviet Government viewed as unequal.

Treaties which addressed spheres of influence in China, the rights of extraterritorial and consular jurisdiction, concessions on Chinese territory, and Russia's share of the indemnities that had been imposed on China by imperialist countries after the suppression of the 'Boxer Rebellion' were declared null and void. Soviet Russia rejected such treaties, regardless of whether they had been concluded with China or with third parties on behalf of China.

These proposals were confirmed in a note dated 27 September 1920 by the People's Commissariat of Foreign Affairs of the RSFSR, which stressed that the Soviet Government would steadfastly adhere to the principles stated in the 25 July 1919 address, and would use them as the basis for a friendship agreement between China and Russia.

The unequal treaties were legally replaced by an agreement, dated 31 May 1934, on the general principles for settling the issues between the USSR and the Chinese Republic.

Neither the 1919 address nor the 1924 agreement between the Soviet Union and the Chinese Republic contained, nor could it have contained, any indications that the treaties that defined the current Sino-Soviet border were among the unequal or secret treaties. Naturally, there was no talk about annulling or re-examining them.

Until recently, the leaders of the PRC themselves stressed that the Soviet State replaced the unequal treaties with China. Mao Zedong announced at the VII CPC Congress in 1945, and repeated again on 16 December 1949, that 'the Soviet Union was the first to reject the unequal treaties and conclude new, fair treaties with China.' Now, however, judging by the Chinese announcement, those who formulate China's policies give priority not to Lenin's decrees, which put an end to the unequal treaties, but to the campaigns of Genghis Khan, Kangxi, and other feudal lords who are being exalted as 'great statesmen and commanders.'

In order to lend a semblance of credibility to its statements about the 'inequality' of the border treaties between China and Russia, the Chinese government is resorting even to tampering with quotes from classics of Marxism-Leninism. It is wilfully manipulating statements taken out of their historical context, which were aimed against the policies of tsarist Russia. For example, a quotation from Lenin's article, 'The Chinese War,' in which the participation of tsarism, together with other imperialist powers, in the suppression of the 'Boxer Rebellion' (the popular uprising of the yihetuans in 1900[4]) was denounced, is cited as 'proof' of the thesis of the 'inequality' of the Treaty of Aigun and Treaty of Peking, which were concluded 40 years before, and about which there is not a single word in Lenin's article.

It is common knowledge that after the end of the Great October Socialist Revolution in 1917, the people of the Soviet Union and the Soviet Government not only put an end to the policy of subjugation, which was conducted by tsarist Russia with respect to the people of the East, but also, through their historical acts and practical affairs, were an example to mankind of a completely new class policy that responded to the interests of the workers of all countries. Not in a single document of the Soviet State, nor in a single one of Lenin's announcements is there a reference to the treaties being unequal or to their being subject to re-examination.

The struggle, under Lenin's leadership, to liberate the Far East from Japanese and other invaders will be inscribed forever in the chronicles of the heroic deeds of our people. The Soviet Union interdicted attempts by the Chinese militarists in Manchuria who encroached our borders, and the Japanese aggressors who wanted to test our will and intransigence in defending the Soviet socialist Fatherland.

It was far from accidental, of course, that the 24 May announcement by the PRC government carefully avoided everything that concerned the expansionist, anti-popular policies of the Chinese bogdykhans. Casting aside the class approach in assessing social phenomena, the PRC government is essentially trying to prove that some feudal conquerors and oppressors – the Chinese – were just, and others – unjust – and to conclude that, together with the collapse of tsarist autocracy, the borders of the Russian state should have crumbled as well.

If we accept the principle advocated in the PRC government announcement, according to which the nationality of territories is determined not by the people who are settled there, but rather by memories of past campaigns, then Latin America obviously would return to the authority of the Spanish crown and the US would return to the bosom of Great Britain. Greece, as the successor of Alexander the Great, could probably demand for itself today's Turkey, Syria, Iran, India, Pakistan, the UAR, etc.

Until recently the PRC government understood what could happen with interstate relations if such an issue were raised. For example, in October 1960, Premier of the State Council Zhou Enlai declared: 'If everyone began to settle scores that go back to the distant past, then chaos would arise in the world.' It is apparent that today China holds the opposite point of view on this subject.

In fact, no territorial issue exists between the Soviet Union and China. There has not been and there cannot be talk about any disruption of the existing situation on the border or any 'seizure of Chinese territory' by the Soviets. For 50 years the Soviet people and their Armed Forces have been protecting the same borders of our country on the Amur and Ussuri Rivers, at Pamir and Tian Shan. These borders are inviolable today, as they were yesterday as well. Any attempt to cross the Soviet border will be devastatingly repelled.

The Soviet Government cannot ignore the fact that the 24 May announcement by the PRC government – as, in fact, many other PRC state documents – contains many libellous fabrications and false attacks that insult the Soviet State and the Soviet people. The USSR government considers it undignified to refute such fictions. The insult and abuse with which the announcement by the PRC government abounds can hardly be viewed as a sincere desire on the part of the Chinese to find a constructive solution to the contentious issues.

In this regard, the Soviet Government cannot fail to focus attention on the fact that the provocations organised by the Chinese authorities on the Soviet border continue. At the same time, PRC officials and organs have unleashed an unbridled anti-Soviet campaign that currently is sweeping over Chinese towns and villages. China's entire propaganda machine has been set in motion to fan anti-Soviet feelings, so as to convince the Chinese population that the Soviet Union wants to attack China. The absurdity of such statements is obvious. All honourable people know that the Soviet people are engaged in peaceful, creative labour, are building communism, and that they have not attacked and do not intend to attack anyone.

III.

The policies of the USSR with regard to the Chinese people were and remain unchanged: they are built on a long-term foundation. We remember that the fundamental interests of the Soviet and Chinese people coincide. The Soviet Union is for good-neighbourliness and friendship with China, and for eliminating everything that could complicate relations between our two states. The Soviet Government contraposes Lenin's internationalist policies of friendship, solidarity, and cooperation to those who sow strife between the Soviet and Chinese people. The unity and cohesion of peace-loving forces advocating social and national liberation are the key to their victories against the threats and direct attacks of imperialism.

The Soviet Government has addressed the PRC government several times with proposals for the normalisation of relations between both countries. This question was raised more than once to the Chinese, in particular, in February 1965 and in March 1966, when it was suggested to conduct a high-level bilateral meeting to discuss in detail all contentious issues.

In its 29 March Announcement, the USSR Government proposed to renew consultations between representatives from the Soviet Union and China to discuss the issue of clarifying the borderline on individual sectors of the border, based on border treaties that are in force. Now it is once again proposing that consultations be conducted, without, of course, any preconditions.

The Soviets support the following: to establish a consensus regarding border sectors for which there are no disagreements; with regard to individual sectors where there are disagreements, to come to an understanding of where the borderline runs by means of mutual consultations on the basis of treaties; with regard to sectors that are subject to natural changes, to proceed from treaties that are in force when determining the borderline, observing the principle of mutual concessions and the economic interests of the local population in these sectors; to fix an agreement, with both sides signing the appropriate documents.

The Soviets agree with the opinion of the PRC government that 'if there is a prerequisite, where treaties on the current Sino-Soviet border are taken as the basis, the necessary settlement may be adjusted in individual border sectors, based on the principles of consultations on an equal footing, mutual understanding, and mutual accommodation.'

The USSR Government is proceeding from the fact that, in order to now create an atmosphere for a pragmatic and constructive discussion of the issues at forthcoming consultations, it is necessary to exclude everything that obstructs the achievement of this goal. In this regard, it is treating with understanding the ideas contained in the PRC government's declaration that the sides avoid conflicts on the border and that their border guards do not resort to weapons in the fulfilment of their duties and not open fire against each other, but rather resolve problems that arise when guarding the existing state border only by peaceful means. It is equally necessary to completely preclude border violation incidents by the sides, no matter what the pretext. Soviet border guards and civilians are strictly observing this policy. The USSR Government expresses the hope that the Chinese border guards and civilians will also be given corresponding instructions.

The Soviet Government proposes that the consultations that were suspended in 1964 be renewed in Moscow in the next two or three months. A specific date can be agreed upon through diplomatic channels. P.I. Zyryanov, the authorised representative of the USSR,

with the rank of deputy minister, has been named the head of the delegation for the consultations.

The Soviet Government expects the PRC government to report in the near future whether the above-mentioned proposals on the time and place for continuing consultation are acceptable.

If the PRC government is ready to normalise the situation on the Sino-Soviet border, the path for this is open.

13 June 1969[5]

APPENDIX II

NOTE FROM THE SOVIET GOVERNMENT TO THE GOVERNMENT OF THE PRC

The Soviet government declares the following to the government of the People's Republic of China.

On 2 March at 4 hours and 10 minutes Moscow time, the Chinese authorities organised an armed provocation on the Sino-Soviet border in the area of the Nizhne-Mikhaylovka border post (Damansky Island) on the Ussuri River. A Chinese detachment crossed the Soviet state border and set off for Damansky Island. According to Soviet border guards who were patrolling this area, the Chinese suddenly opened fire from machine guns and automatic weapons. The actions of the Chinese border violators were supported by fire from an ambush on the Chinese bank of the Ussuri River. More than 200 Chinese soldiers took part in this confrontational attack against the Soviet border guards. As a result of this bandit raid, there were dead and wounded Soviet border guards.

The naked armed incursion into Soviet territory is a provocation organised by Chinese authorities and pursues the goal of exacerbating the situation on the Sino-Soviet border.

The Soviet government is lodging a resolute protest to the government of the People's Republic of China because of the

dangerous provocative actions of the Chinese authorities on the Sino-Soviet border.

The Soviet government demands a swift investigation of and severest punishment for those persons responsible for organising this provocation. It insists that immediate measures be taken to preclude any violation of the Sino-Soviet border.

The Soviet government reserves the right to take decisive measures to interdict provocations on the Sino-Soviet border and warns the government of the People's Republic of China that all responsibility for possible consequences of opportunistic policies aimed at exacerbating the situation on the borders between China and the Soviet Union lies with the government of the People's Republic of China.

The Soviet government is guided by feelings of friendship in relations with the Chinese people, and it intends to continue to follow this line. We will, however, repel and decisively interdict reckless provocative actions by the Chinese authorities.

Moscow, 2 March 1969[1]

APPENDIX III

ANNOUNCEMENT BY L.M. ZAMYATIN, HEAD OF THE PRESS DEPARTMENT OF THE USSR MFA AT A PRESS CONFERENCE FOR SOVIET AND FOREIGN JOURNALISTS, HELD ON 7 MARCH 1969

The armed provocation by Chinese authorities on the Sino-Soviet border has caused the justified anger and outrage of all Soviet people. The blatant bandit raid against Soviet border guards has been perceived everywhere in the world as one more new manifestation of the unprincipled actions of the current Chinese leadership and its irresponsible playing with the lives of people for the sake of its plans and calculations.

Following the tested procedures of international provocateurs, the Chinese authorities are attempting to distort the facts, disclaim responsibility for the provocation that was undertaken, and shift the responsibility onto the Soviet Union. They want to convince their people that the Chinese were not to blame for the blood that was spilled on the Ussuri River. Facts, however, are facts, no matter how Peking tries to alter them. This is how, in fact, everything happened.

On the night of 2 March, around 300 armed Chinese soldiers violated the Soviet state border and went across the channel of the Ussuri River to the Soviet Damansky Island. Dressed in white camouflage smocks and spread out on this island in the forest and bushes behind natural raised terrain, this group set up an ambush. Military subunits and fire resources – mortars, grenade launchers, and heavy machine guns – were concentrated on the Chinese bank of the Ussuri River. Field telephone lines had been laid between the group that landed on Damansky Island and the military subunits on the Chinese riverbank.

At 4 hours and 10 minutes, another 30 armed Chinese violators set off from the Chinese riverbank across the USSR state border toward Damansky Island. A group of Soviet border guards, headed by Senior Lieutenant Strelnikov, the chief of the outpost, arrived across the ice of the Ussuri River at the scene of the border violation.

As before, the Soviet border guards intended to protest to the Chinese about the border violation and drive them from the territory of the Soviet Union. Fire was treacherously opened against the Soviet border guards, and the Chinese provocateurs literally shot at point blank range. Artillery and mortar fire was opened from the Chinese riverbank against another group of Soviet border guards.

Together with reinforcements that had arrived from the neighbouring border post, the Soviet border guards exhibited courage, bravery, and valour and decisively drove the violators from Soviet territory.

The facts show that the Chinese provocation in the area of Damansky Island was deliberately planned beforehand. It was carried out by army subunit forces that had been specially trained for this provocation. An examination of Soviet territory at the scene of the battle discovered mine tail fins, shell and grenade fragments, and Chinese weapons and military equipment left behind during the flight.

During the provocation, the Chinese military committed incredibly brutal and cruel acts against the wounded Soviet border guards. Based on the on-site inspection and the conclusions of the medical commission, which examined the corpses of the dead Soviet border guards, it can be stated that the wounded were shot by the Chinese at close range [and/or] stabbed with bayonets. The faces of some of the dead border guards were distorted beyond recognition. The actions of the Chinese regarding the Soviet border guards can be compared only with the most fanatical savagery of the Chinese militarists and followers of Chang Kai Shek in the 1920s–1930s during armed conflicts. The bandit raid organised by the Chinese authorities cost the lives of 31 Soviet border guards, with another 14 men being wounded. The Soviet border guards bravely and selflessly fulfilled their military duty to defend the inviolability of the borders of their Soviet socialist Motherland.

Following the armed incursion into Soviet territory, on cue a new wave of anti-Soviet hysteria and nationalist psychosis was raised in China. Anti-Soviet slogans and threats can be heard at organised rallies attended by large crowds. Since 3 March the Soviet embassy in Peking has been subjected to a siege, in the full sense of the word, by hooligan groups.

Why did Mao Zedong's group need this armed provocation and its accompanying political coven?

These criminal actions by Mao Zedong's group are pursuing far-reaching goals. The Maoists are attempting to create an atmosphere in their country that would make it possible for them to distract the attention of the Chinese people from the enormous economic and political failures within the country and make it possible to consolidate Mao Zedong's risky great-power course, which is aimed at the further exacerbation of relations with socialist and other peace-loving countries.

Of course, it is not by chance that the provocation on the Sino-Soviet border was carried out during the preparation of the IX Conference of the CPC. It was apparently calculated that in a situation of anti-Soviet hysteria it would be easier to foist on the congress a platform that was hostile to the Soviet Union and CPSU and to legitimise anti-Sovietism as its state policy.

Of course, there are circles in the world that try to use this kind of provocation to their advantage. It cannot be considered accidental that the armed bandit raid in the area of Damansky Island resonated with the reactionary circles of the United States of America and in West Germany, which have begun to estimate out loud what they could gain from tension on the Sino-Soviet border.

The Soviet people have not equated and do not equate Mao Zedong's group with the Chinese people. Our country has always been guided and is guided by feelings of friendship with regard to the Chinese people. However, as was pointed out in the note from the Soviet government to the government of the PRC, thoughtless provocative actions by the Chinese authorities will be met by us with the necessary response and be decisively interdicted. All responsibility for possible consequences of this risky policy by China's leadership, aimed at exacerbating the situation on the border between China and the Soviet Union and on aggravating relations between our countries, lies on the government of the People's Republic of China.[1]

APPENDIX IV[1]

SOVIET REPORT TO EAST GERMAN LEADERSHIP ON SINO-SOVIET BORDER CLASHES

5 Copies
3/8/69
On March 2 1969, at 11 o'clock local time, the Chinese organized [sic] a provocation on the Island Damansky, which is located on the river Ussuri south of Khabarovsk, between the points Bikin and Iman (Primorsky Region).

The ascertained facts are that this action had been prepared by the Chinese government for a long time. In December 1968 and in January/February 1969, groups of armed Chinese soldiers violated the border at the Damansky Island several times, operating from Hunzy. After protests by the Soviet border guards, the Chinese military returned to their border posts or marched along the line which constitutes the border between China and the USSR.

In the events of March 2, 1969, the border control forces at Hunzy played only a secondary role. An especially trained unit of the Chinese People's Liberation Army with a force of more than 200 men was used for the staging of this provocation. Secretly, this unit was brought on the Island Damansky during the night of March 2. The men in this unit had special gear and wore camouflage clothes. A telephone line to the unit was installed from the Chinese shore. Prior to this, reserves and munitions, among others PAC batteries, mines, and armored [sic] artillery and heavy fire guns, had been pulled together near the Chinese shore. The stabilizers [sic], shelling, mines, and grenade splinters, and the kind of crates left in the tanks that were hit, found later provided the proof that these weapons had indeed been used.

Around 2 o'clock Moscow time (9 o'clock local time) our observation posts noted the advance of 30 armed Chinese military men on the Island of Damansky. Consequently, a group of Soviet border guards was dispatched to the location where the Chinese had violated the border. The officer in charge of the unit and a small contingent approached the border violators with the intention of registering protests and demanding (without using force) that they leave Soviet territory, as had been done repeatedly in the past. But within the first minutes of the exchange, our border guards came under crossfire and were insidiously shot without any warning. At the same time, fire on the remaining parts of our force was opened from an ambush on the island and from the Chinese shore. The guards then assumed combat order, and, reinforced by the approaching reserve from the nearby border post, threw back the Chinese surprise attack, and expelled them through decisive action from Soviet territory.

There were casualties and wounded men on both sides.

When the location of the island where the incident had happened was inspected, military equipment, telephones, and phone lines connecting to the Chinese mainland, as well as large numbers of scattered empty liquor bottles (which had obviously been used by the Chinese provocateurs and the participants in this adventure beforehand to gain courage) were found.

There are no settlements on the Island of Damansky and it is of no economic importance at all; there are no villages in the vicinity for dozens of miles. One can obviously draw the conclusion that it [the island] was chosen as the site for the provocation because such an endeavor [sic] could be prepared there secretly and then presented to the world in a version advantageous to the organizers [sic].

During the provocation, the Chinese military committed incredibly brutal and cruel acts against the wounded Soviet border guards. Based on the on-site inspection and the expert knowledge of the medical commission which examined the bodies of the dead Soviet border guards, it can be stated that the wounded were shot by the Chinese from close range [and/or] stabbed with bayonets and knifes [sic]. The faces of some of the casualties were distorted beyond recognition, others had their uniforms and boots taken off by the Chinese. The cruelties committed by the Chinese toward the Soviet border guards can only be compared with the worst brutalities of the Chinese militarists and Chiang Kai-Shek's [Jiang Jieshi's] men during the '20s and '30s.

The crime by the Mao Zedong group which caused loss of lives has far-reaching objectives.

The Maoists exacerbate the anti-Soviet hysteria and produce a chauvinist frenzy in the country, creating an atmosphere which enables them to establish Mao Zedong's anti-Soviet and chauvinist-great power course as the general line of the Chinese policy at the IX Party Convention of the CPC.

It is also obvious that the Mao group has the intention of using the anti-Soviet psychosis it created for its subversive and divisive policy in the international Communist movement. The Maoists apparently strive to make an all-out effort to complicate and prevent the convention of the International Consultation of Communist and Workers' Parties in order to create distrust in the Soviet Union and the CCPU among the fraternal parties.

The new dangerous provocations of the Maoists reveal Beijing's intention to activate the opportunistic political flirtation with the imperialist countries – above all with the United States and West Germany. It is no accident that the ambush on the Soviet border unit was staged by the Chinese agencies at a time when Bonn started its provocation of holding the election of the Federal President in West Berlin.

The provocation in the area of the Island of Damansky is part of the Maoists' policy which aims at forcing a radical reversal in the foreign and domestic policies of the PR [People's Republic] of China and at transforming the country de facto into a power hostile toward the socialist countries.

The Mao Zedong group has prepared the organization [sic] of armed provocations along the Soviet-Chinese border for a long time. The Chinese authorities have been creating artificial tensions at the Soviet-Chinese border since 1960. Since this time the Chinese have undertaken several thousand border violations with provocative goals.

At the beginning of 1967, the number of border violations by Chinese authorities increased sharply. In some districts they tried to install demonstratively border patrols on the islands and those parts of the rivers belonging to the USSR. In December 1967 and in January 1968, the Chinese undertook large provocative actions on the island of Kirkinsi [sic] on the Ussuri [River] and in the area of the Kasakevich Canal. On January 23, 1969, the Chinese staged an armed attack on the island of Damansky.

The border in the area of the Island of Damansky was established according to the Treaty of Beijing of 1860 and the enclosed map which the representatives of Russia and China signed in June 1863. According to the then drawn-up demarcation line the Island of Damansky is located on the territory of the USSR. This line has always been protected by Soviet border guards.

Confronted with the Chinese provocations at the border, the Soviet side, for years, has taken active steps towards a regulation of the situation.

The question of the borderline was discussed in the bilateral Soviet-Chinese Consultations on the Determination of the Borderline in Certain Controversial Areas of 1964. The Soviet side made a number of proposals regarding the examination of the controversial border question. The Chinese leadership, however, was determined to let these consultations fail. The Chinese delegation put up the completely untenable demand to recognize [sic] the unequal character of the treaties delineating the Soviet-Chinese border and raised territorial claims against the Soviet Union about an area of altogether 1,575,000 square kilometers [sic]. On July 10, 1964, Mao Zedong declared in a conversation with Japanese members of parliament with regard to the Chinese territorial demands against the Soviet Union that "we have not yet presented the bill for this territory."

On August 22, 1964, the consultations were interrupted. Despite our repeated proposals the Chinese did not resume the conversations and did not react even when the question was mentioned in the Soviet foreign ministry note of August 31, 1967.

Meanwhile the Chinese authorities continued to violate grossly the Soviet-Chinese agreement of 1951 on the regulation of the navigation in the border rivers. In 1967 and 1968 they blew up the consultations of the mixed Soviet-Chinese navigation commission which had been established on the basis of the agreement of 1951.

In the Chinese border areas large military preparations set in (construction of airports, access routes, barracks and depots, training of militia, etc.).

The Chinese authorities conspicuously conjure up situations of conflict along the border and stage provocations there. On our part, all measures have been taken to avoid an escalation of the situation and to prevent incidents and conflicts. The Soviet border troops have been instructed not to use their arms and, if possible, to avoid armed collisions. The instruction on the non-use of arms was strictly enforced, although the Chinese acted extremely provocatively in many cases, employed the most deceitful tricks, picked fights, and attacked our border guards with stabbing weapons, with steel rod, and other such things.

The armed provocation in the area of the Island of Damansky is a logical consequence of this course of the Chinese authorities and is part of a far-reaching plan by Beijing aiming at increasing the Maoists' anti-Soviet campaign.

Since March 3, 1969, the Soviet Embassy in Beijing has been exposed again to an organized [*sic*] siege by specially trained groups of Maoists. Brutal acts of force and rowdylike excesses again the representatives of Soviet institutions are occurring throughout China every day. All over the country, an unbridled anti-Soviet campaign has been kindled. It is characteristic that this whole campaign assumed a military coloration, that an atmosphere of chauvinistic frenzy has been created throughout the country.

Faced with this situation the CC of the CPSU and the Soviet government are undertaking the necessary steps to prevent further border violations. They will do everything necessary in order to frustrate the criminal intentions of the Mao Zedong group which are to create hostility between the Soviet people and the Chinese people.

The Soviet Government is led in its relations with the Chinese people by feelings of friendship and is intent on pursuing this policy in the future. Ill-considered provocative actions of the Chinese authorities will, however, be decisively repudiated on our part and brought to an end with determination.

BIBLIOGRAPHY

Books

Anon., *Collection of Treaties between Russia and Other States. 1856-1917* (Сборник договоров России с другими государствами. 1856-1917 [in Russian]) (Moscow: Publisher unknown, 1952)

Anon., *Learn from the Battle Heroes of Zhenbao Island* (Учитесь у боевых героев Острова Чжэеньбао, [in Russian, translated from Chinese]) (Xinhua Bookstore of Liaoning Province, Liaoning People's Art Printing Factory, 1970)

Anon., *Russia's Border Troops in Wars and Military Conflicts of the 20th Century* (Пограничные войска в войнах и вооруженных конфликтах XX века [in Russian]) (Moscow: Granitsa, 2000)

Belyavskaya, V.F. (author-compiler), *Border Guards* (Пограничники [in Russian]) (Minsk: Literatura, 1998)

Brezhnev, A.A., *China: The Thorny Path to Good Neighbourliness* (Китай: тернистый путь к добрососедству [in Russian]) (Moscow: Mezhdunarodnye otnosheniya, 1998)

Bubenin, V.D., *The Bloody Snow of Damansky* (Кровавый снег Даманского [in Russian]) (Moscow: Kuchkove pole, 2004)

Defense Intelligence Agency, *Handbook of the Chinese People's Liberation Army*, DDB-2680-32-84, 1984

Drozdov, Yu.I., *Notes from a Chief of Illegal Intelligence* (Записки нацчальника нелегальной разведки [in Russian]) (Moscow: Olma-Press, 2000)

Galenovich, Yu.M., *Russia and China in the 20th Century. The Border* (Россия и Китай в XX веке. Граница [in Russian]) (Moscow: Izograf, 2001)

Galenovich, Yu.M., *Russia—China: Six Treaties* (Россия–Китай: шесть договоров [in Russian]) (Moscow: Muravey, 2003)

Gladkov, V. and Musalov, A., *The Uneasy Border. 1969* (Неспокойная граница. Год 1969-й [in Russian]), (Moscow: Granitsa, 2018)

Kapitsa, M.S., *At Different Parallels. Notes of a Diplomat* (На разных параллелях. Записки дипломата [in Russian]) (Moscow: AO "Kniga i biznes," 1996)

Kholmogorov, M. (compiler), *Heroes of Damansky Island* (Герои острова Даманский [in Russian]) (Moscow: Molodaya gvardiya, 1969)

Leonova, Ye.D and Murin, V.B., *Demokrat Leonov: a Life in the Name of Duty* (Демократ Леонов: жизнь во имя долга [in Russian]) (Moscow: Granitsa, 2016)

Lukashin, V., *The Heroes of Damansky* (Герои Даманского [in Russian]) (Moscow: Izvestiya, 1969)

Ministry of Defense of the USSR, *Soviet Military Encyclopaedia* (Советская военная энциклопедия [in Russian]), Vol. 3 (Moscow: Voyenizdat, 1979)

Musalov, A., *Damansky and Zhalanashkol. The 1969 Sino-Soviet Armed Conflict* (Даманский и Жаланашколь. Советско-китайский вооруженный конфликт 1969 года [in Russian]) (Moscow: Izdatelskii tsentr 'Eksprint,' 2005)

Petrov, I.I., *The Sino-Soviet Wars. The Truth about Damansky* (Советско-китайские войны. Правда о Даманском [in Russian]) (Moscow: 'Eksmo': 'Yauza,' 2009)

Razmazin, P., *Damansky. Our Pain. Sorrow. Memory. ..* (Даманский. Наша боль. Скорбь. Память. .. [in Russian]), a project of P. Razmazin (Dalnerechensk: B.M.I., 1999)

Robinson, Thomas, 'The People's Republic. Part 2. Revolutions within the Chinese Revolution, 1966-1982,' in various authors, *The Cambridge History of China*, (Cambridge University Press: Cambridge, 1992) Vol. 15

Robinson, T. W., *The Sino-Soviet Border Dispute: Background, Development, and the March 1969 Clashes*, Rand Corporation Research Memorandum RM-6171-PR, 1970.

Ryabushkin, D.S., *Damansky Island. The Border Conflict. March 1969* (Остров Даманский. Пограничный конфликт. Март 1969 года [in Russian]) (Moscow: Fond 'Russkiye Vityazi,' 2015)

Ryabushkin, D.S., *It Was on Damansky* (Это было на Даманском [in Russian]) (Kazan: Book, 2019)

Ryabushkin, D.S., *Myths of Damansky* (Мифы Даманского [in Russian]) (Moscow: AST, 2004)

Ryabushkin, D.S., 'Origins and Consequences of the Soviet–Chinese Border Conflict of 1969,' in Akihiro, Iwashita, *Eager Eyes Fixed on Eurasia* (Sapporo: Slavic Research Center, Hokkaido University, 2007), pp.73–91

Sabadash, A.A. et al., *Transcripts of Conversations with Veterans of the War on Damansky Island V.I. Abramov, A.S. Belozerov, M.T. Vashchenko, G.A. Kuzminykh, N.I. Никифоров, V.S. Prosvirnikov, N.I. Ruban, V.P. Fateyev, A.I. Filimonov, 2002-2003* (Стенограммы бесед с участниками конфликта на острове Даманском В.И. Абрамовым, А.С. Белозеровым, М.Т. Ващенко, Г.А. Кузьминых, Н.И. Никифоровым, В.С. Просвирниковым, Н.И. Рубаном, В.П. Фатеевым, А. И. Филимоновым, 2003-2004 [in Russian]) (unpublished)

Streltsov, D.V. (ed.), *The Territorial Issue in the Afro-Asian World* (Территориальный вопрос в афро-азиатском мире [in Russian]) (Moscow: Aspect Press, 2013)

Sviderskiy, N.G., 'Facets of Character' (Грани характера [in Russian]), in Anon., *Heroes of the Far Eastern Borders (Collection of Materials on the Defenders of Damansky Island)* (Герои рубежей дальневосточных (Сборник материалов о защитниках острова Даманский) [in Russian]) (Khabarovsk: Publisher unknown, 1969)

Vashchenko, M.T. and Knyazev, A.L., (compilers), *Island of Bravery. Recollections of Veterans of the Combat Operations on Damansky Island* (Остров мужества. Воспоминания участников боевых действий на о. Даманский [in Russian]) (Khabarovsk: izdatel'stvo 'RIOTIP' kraevoy tipografii, 2006)

Yakovets, A.P., (compiler), *Damansky. This Is How It Was. The 50th Anniversary of the Border Conflict on the Ussuri River. 1969-2019* (Даманский. Так это было. 50 лет пограничному конфликту на реке Уссури. 1969-2019 [in Russian]), 2nd edition, corrected and supplemented: album (Vladivostok: Russkii ostrov, 2019)

Zhibin, Chen and Xiaozhu, Sun, *Confrontation at the Freezing Point: Record of the 1962-1969 Sino-Soviet Border Battles* (Конфронтация при замораживании: запись советско-китайской пограничной битвы с 1962 по 1969 год [in Russian, translated from Chinese]) (Beijing: International Cultural Publication Company, 1992)

Zhisui, Li, *Notes of a Personal Physician* (Записки личного врача [in Russian]), Book 1 (Minsk: Inter-Digest, Smolensk: TOO Ekho, 1996)

Periodical Articles

Anon., 'Damansky – Land of Heroes' (Даманский – земля героев [in Russian]), *Starshina – Serzhant*, 5 (1969), pp.4–7

Anon., 'The Red Ice of the Ussuri' (Красный лед Уссури [in Russian]), *Vostok Rossii*, 10:32 (1992), pp.8–9

Burr, W., 'Sino-American Relations. 1969: The Sino-Soviet Border War and Steps Towards Rapprochement,' *Cold War History*, 1:3 (2001), pp.73–112

Danhui, Li 'Sino-Soviet Border Conflicts in 1969: Causes and Effects' [in Chinese], *Dangdai zhongguoshi yanjiu*, 3 (1996), pp.39–50.

Fridyev, V. 'A Border of Living Hearts,' (Граница живых сердец [in Russian]), *Okeanskiye vesti*, 17 (1999)

Goldstein, Lyle, 'Return to Zhenbao Island: Who Started Shooting and Why It Matters,' *The China Quarterly*, 168 (December 2001), pp.985–997

Jun, Niu, Baijia, Zhang and others, '1966–1976: Isolation is Replaced by Openness' (1966–1976: Изоляция сменяется открытостью [in Russian]), *Mirovye znaniya*, 13:1 July (2006), pp.19-22 (translated from Chinese by D.V. Kiselev)

Koleshnya, M.I. 'Damansky Island, 1969' (Остров Даманский, год 1969 [in Russian]), *Rossiya i ATR*, 2 (1999), pp.86–87.

Kuisong, Yang, 'The Sino-Soviet Border Clash of 1969: From Zhenbao Island to Sino-American Rapprochement,' *Cold War History*, 1:1 (2000), pp.21–53

Mizhou, Hui 'Sino-Soviet Battles on the Border' (Русско-китайские побоища на границе [in Russian]), *Кempo*, 1997, No.2 (34), pp.5–6

Ostermann, S.F., "East German Documents on the Sino-Soviet Border Conflict, 1969," *The Cold War in Asia, Cold War International History Project Bulletin*, Issues 6–7 (1995/96), pp.186–193

Pankov, Yu. and Ryskin, A., 'Secret Island: What Happened on Damansky in March 1969?' (Таинственный остров: Что происходило на Даманском в марте 1969? [in Russian]), *Molodoy Dalnevostochnik*, 15 December 1990

Ryabushkin, D.S., 'Damansky Island, 2 March 1969' (Остров Даманский, 2 марта 1969 года [in Russian]), *Voprosy istorii*, 5 (2004), pp.148–152

Ryabushkin, D.S., 'How Did the Events on Damansky Island End (Чем завершилось события на острове Даманском [in Russian]), *Voprosy istorii*, 12 (2005), pp. 168–170

Ryabushkin, D.S., 'It Was on Damanskii Island,' *The Journal of Slavic Military Studies*, 31:4 (2018), pp.1–16

Ryabushkin, D.S., 'The Myths of Damanskii Island (1969),' *The Journal of Slavic Military Studies*, 16:3 (2003), pp.149–172

Ryabushkin, D.S., 'New Documents on the Sino-Soviet Ussuri Border Clashes,' *Eurasia Border Review*, 3 (2012), pp.161–174

Ryabushkin, D.S., 'What They Fought with on Damanskii Island,' *The Journal of Slavic Military Studies*, 19 (2006), pp.149–166

Ryabushkin, D.S., and Pavliuk, V.D., 'Soviet Artillery in the Battles for Damanskii Island,' *The Journal of Slavic Military Studies*, 20:1 (2007), pp.121–134

Vashchenko, G.T., 'Damansky: (History of the Origin of the Name Damansky Island. About Engineer S.I. Damansky)' (Даманский: (История происхождения назв. о-ва Даманский. Об инженере С.И. Даманском)[in Russian]), *Suvorovskii natisk*, 11 August 1998, p.6

Verlin, Ye, 'For Generations to Come' (На поколения вперед [in Russian]), *Ekspert*, No. 27:238 (2000), p.36

Pamphlets

Anon., 'Down with the New Tsars!', Foreign Languages Press, Peking, 1969

Internet Sites

Anon., 'Border Conflicts and Disputes' (Приграничные конфликты и споры [in Russian]) <http://magazines.russ.ru/oz/2002/6/2002_06_27.html> (date accessed: 6 September 2020)

Anon., 'The Dulaty Operation' (Дулатинская операция [in Russian]), <https://pikabu.ru/story/dulatinskaya_operatsiya_6429090> (date accessed: 4 October 2020)

Anon., 'Border Conflicts and Disputes' (fragment published in the Journal *Fatherland Notes* (Пограничные конфликты и споры <фрагмент>, опубликовано в журнале *Отечественные записки* [in Russian]), No. 6 (2002) <http://magazines.russ.ru/oz/2002/6/2002_06_27.html> (date accessed: 4 October 2020)

Anon., 'From the History of a Great Friendship' (Из истории великой дружбы [in Russian]), *Kommersant–Vlast*, 8:309 (1999), pp.10–14. <https://www.kommersant.ru/doc/15227> (date accessed: 6 September 2020)

Department of State. Memorandum of Conversation, August 18, 1969, <https://nsarchive2.gwu.edu/NSAEBB/NSAEBB49/sino.sov.10.pdf> (date accessed: 19 September 2020)

Khrushchev, Nikita *Time, People, Power* (Время. Люди. Власть [in Russian]) <http://www.hrono.ru/libris/lib_h/hrush50.html> (date accessed: 7 September 2020)

Note of Ministry of Foreign Affairs of China, 2 March 1960 <https://books.google.com/books?id=jH3zAAAAMAAJ&pg=PA174&lpg=PA174&dq=Note+of+Ministry+of+Foreign+Affairs+of+China+2+March+1969&source=bl&ots=7qF39zRpPR&sig=ACfU3U3L9kmkzlz9YMcHL7uWUOBxUB3W4Q&hl=en&sa=X&ved=2ahUKEwjYoIa3rPnoAhUK0qYKHfoqBc4Q6AEwAXoECAoQAQ#v=onepage &q=Note%20of%20Ministry%20of%20Foreign% 20Affairs%20of%20China%202%20March%201969 &f=false> (date accessed: 26 September 2020)

Plugatarev, I., 'Chinese Glory of Damansky Island' (Китайская слава острова Даманский [in Russian]), *Nezavisimoye voyennoye obozreniye*, 27 March 2009 (<http://nvo.ng.ru/realty/2009-03-27/10_damanskiy.html> (date accessed: 24 September 2020))

Secretary of State. Memorandum for the President. Possibility of a Soviet Strike against Chinese Nuclear Facilities. September 10, 1969. <https://nsarchive2.gwu.edu/NSAEBB/NSAEBB49/sino.sov.19.pdf> (date accessed: 19 September 2020)

Xinren, Mao, 'Truth and Fiction about the Border Conflict on Damansky Island: the USSR and China Had to Pay Dearly' (Правда и вымысел о пограничном конфликте на острове Даманский: СССР и Китаю пришлось дорого заплатить [in Russian]) <https://inosmi.ru/social/20190317/244762270.html> (date accessed: 30 September 2020)

<http://asiapacific.narod.ru> (date accessed: 10 September 2019)

<http://citynews.tula.ru/baz/news/tk/tk020613/tk12_1.html> (date accessed: 12 June 2018)

<http://elite-soldiers.by.ru/istor8.htm> (date accessed: 1 April 2019)

<http://extend.hk.hi.cn/~daikang/junshi/zbdz.htm> (date accessed: 12 August 2019)

<http://nbp.gok.ru/Limonka/178_12_2.htm> (date accessed: 16 September 2015)

<http://wemedia.ifeng.com/49968791/wemedia.shtml> (date accessed: 12 August 2019)

<http://www.damanski-zhenbao.ru> (date accessed: 17 March 2015)

<http://www.damanski-zhenbao.ru/files/arhi-17-rus.doc> (date accessed: 27 March 2015)

<http://www.gwu.edu/nsarchiv/NSAEBB/NSAEBB49> (date accessed: 19 September 2020)

<http://www.khabenergo.ru/rus/news/press_17-03.html> (date accessed: 11 September 2020)

<http://www.maoism.ru> (date accessed: 2 August 2019)

< https://rikabu.ru/story/dulatinskaya_operatsiya_6429090> (date accessed: 16 May 2020)

<http://www.russ-chinfrien.narod.ru> (date accessed: 6 September 2020)

<https://www.scmp.com/news/china/diplomacy/article/30911611/why-russias-vladivostok-celebration-prompted-nationalist> (date accessed: 10 July 2020)

<www.fmprc.gov.cn> (date accessed: 15 June 2018)

NOTES

Chapter 1

1 Authors' note: Reinforced here means no fewer than 10 men with group weapons (SPG-9 grenade launchers), grenades, and an adequate amount of ammunition.

2 Authors' note: After the events, 45th Corps obtained one more division – 81st Guards MRD from the Kiev Military District.

3 E.D. Leonova and V.B. Murin, *Demokrat Leonov: A Life in the Name of Duty* (Демократ Леонов: жизнь во имя долга [in Russian]) (Moscow: Granitsa, 2016), p.105.

4 P. Razmazin, *Damansky. Our Pain. Sorrow. Memory...* (Даманский. Наша боль. Скорбь. Память. .. [in Russian]), a project of P. Razmazin (Dalnerechensk: B.M.I., 1999), p.9.

5 Leonova and Murin, *Demokrat Leonov: A Life in the Name of Duty*, pp.107–108.

6 V.F. Belyavskaya (author-compiler), *Border Guards* (Пограничники [in Russian]) (Minsk: Publisher unknown, 1998), p.181.

7 Authors' note: For a long time Soviet mass media said that Leonov was moving in an APC. Apparently, they did not want to admit that not only border guards, but also Soviet Army subunits had taken part in the 15 March fighting.

8 *Damansky. Our Pain, Sorrow. Memory*, p.12.

9 Authors' note: The delegation consisted of Chairman of the USSR Council of Ministers A.N. Kosygin, Minister of Defence Marshal A.A. Grechko, Minister of Foreign Affairs A.A. Gromyko, and Secretary of the CC CPSU F.F. Katushev. Some authors mistakenly say that Marshal Grechko was in India. In fact, he had visited India somewhat earlier, during the first days of March.

10 <http://www.khabenergo.ru/rus/news/press_17-03.html> (date accessed: 11 September 2016).

11 A.A. Sabadash et al., *Transcripts of Conversations with Veterans of the War on Damansky Island V.I. Abramov, A.S. Belozerov, M.T. Vashchenko, G.A. Kuzminykh, N.I. Nikiforov, V.S. Prosvirnikov, N.I. Ruban, V.P. Fateyev, A.I. Filimonov, 2002-2003* (Стенограммы бесед с участниками конфликта на острове Даманском В.И. Абрамовым, А.С. Белозеровым, М.Т. Ващенко, Г.А. Кузьминых, Н.И. Никифоровым, В.С. Просвирниковым, Н.И. Рубаном, В.П. Фатеевым, А. И. Филимоновым, 2003-2004 [in Russian]) (unpublished).

12 *Pravda*, 16 March 1969

13 Translator's note: The text of the order is translated word for word, maintaining the style and punctuation.

14 Authors' note: There is apparently a mistake in the order. Some photos clearly show that Orekhov has two stripes on the shoulder of his uniform, indicating that he held the rank of junior sergeant.

15 Translator's note: Orekhov was awarded the Hero of the Soviet Union Medal on 31 July 1969. The aim of Zakharov's order, dated 19 November 1969, was to enter his name forever in the list of his military unit. When a rollcall takes place his name is called, too, and one of the soldiers must proclaim: 'Hero of the Soviet Union Junior Sergeant Orekhov perished in the battle for freedom and independence of our Motherland.'

16 The text of the order was provided by A.A. Sabadash.

17 This information is also from A.A. Sabadash, who cites a certain Kosinsky, a veteran of the battle.

18 M.I. Koleshnya, 'Damansky Island, 1969' (Остров Даманский, год 1969-й [in Russian]), *Rossiya i ATR*, 1999 (2), p.89.

19 Yang Kuisong, 'The Sino-Soviet Border Clash of 1969: From Zhenbao Island to Sino-American Rapprochement,' *Cold War History*, Vol. 1 (1), 2000, pp.25–26.

20 Yang Kuisong, 'The Sino-Soviet Border Clash of 1969,' p.29.

21 Translator's note: the original uses the term 'kroshevo,' literally 'crumb.' Kroshevo is finely chopped dark green upper cabbage leaves that are usually removed from the heads of cabbage when harvesting. Since green leaves are coarser than ordinary cabbage, they are not shredded, but chopped very finely to make crumbs.

22 'From the History of a Great Friendship' (Из истории великой дружбы [in Russian]), *Kommersant-Vlast*, No. 8:309 (1999), <https://www.kommersant.ru/doc/15227> (date accessed: 11 September 2020).

23 <http://nbp.gok.ru/Limonka/178_12_2.htm> (date accessed: 16 September 2015)

24 T.W. Robinson, *The Sino-Soviet Border Dispute: Background, Development, and the March 1969 Clashes* (Rand Corporation, Research Memorandum RM-6171-PR, 1970), pp.38–39. All spellings in citations taken directly from his work reflect the US spelling in the original.

25 Robinson, *The Sino-Soviet Border Dispute*, pp.39–40.

26 Robinson, *The Sino-Soviet Border Dispute*, p.40.

27 Robinson, *The Sino-Soviet Border Dispute*, p.40.

Chapter 2

1 Sabadash, *Transcripts of Conversations with Veterans of the War on Damansky Island*.

2 V. Fridyev, 'A Border of Living Hearts,' (Граница живых сердец [in Russian]), *Okeanskie vesti*, 17 (1999).

3 Anon., 'Damansky – Land of Heroes,' (Даманский – земля героев [in Russian]), *Starshina – serzhant*, 5 (1969), pp.4–7.

Chapter 3

1 Authors' note: Unless otherwise stated, all letters cited in this chapter are from correspondences between author Dmitry Ryabushkin and veterans of the Damansky events.

2 Authors' note: Popov's letters have already been cited in Volume 1 in the discussion about the events after the 2 March battle.

3 Author's note: Unless otherwise indicated, citations in the remainder of this chapter are from M.T. Vashchenko and A.L. Knyazev (compilers), *Island of Bravery. Recollections of Veterans of the Combat Operations on Damansky Island* (Остров мужества. Воспоминания участников боевых действий на о. Даманский [in Russian]) (Khabarovsk: izdatel'stvo 'RIOTIP'kraevoj tipografii, 2006).

4   *Suvorovskiy natisk*, 22 March 1969.

5   Sabadash, et al., *Transcripts of Conversations with Veterans of the War on Damansky Island*.

6   The following excerpt was provided by A. N. Musalov.

Chapter 4

1   Anon., *Learn from the Battle Heroes of Zhenbao Island* (Учитесь у боевых героев Острова Чжэеньбао, [in Russian, translated from Chinese]) (Xinhua Bookstore of Liaoning Province, Liaoning People's Art Printing Factory, 1970). Unless otherwise indicated, all photos in this chapter are found in this source, accessed on the Chinese Internet.

2   <http://wemedia.ifeng.com/49968791/wemedia.shtml> (date accessed: 12 August 2019).

3   <http://extend.hk.hi.cn/~daikang/junshi/zbdz.htm> (date accessed: 12 August 2019).

4   Sun Yuguo and Zhou Dengguo.

5   Authors' note: Ma Xianjie, the chief of 133rd Division's intelligence department, was the commander of the Chinese ambush on Damansky on 2 March 1969.

6   W. Burr, 'Sino-American Relations. 1969. The Sino-Soviet Border War and Steps Toward Rapprochement,' *Cold War History*, 1:3 (2001), pp.73–112.

7   Authors' note: Information about the cemetery and the list of dead Chinese were provided by A.A. Sabadash.

Chapter 5

1   V. Gladkov and A. Musalov, *The Uneasy Border. 1969* (Неспокойная граница. Год 1969-й [in Russian]) (Moscow: Granitsa, 2018), p.158.

2   < https://rikabu.ru/story/dulatinskaya_operatsiya_6429090> (date accessed: 16 May 2020)

3   I.I. Petrov, *The Sino-Soviet Wars. The Truth about Damansky* (Советско-китайские войны. Правда о Даманском [in Russian]) (Moscow: 'Eksmo': 'Yauza,' 2009), p.123.

4   *Pravda*, 12 June 1969.

5   *Pravda*, 9 July 1969.

6   A.P. Yakovets (compiler), *Damansky. This Is How It Was. The 50th Anniversary of the Border Conflict on the Ussuri River. 1969-2019* (Даманский. Так это было. 50 лет пограничному конфликту на реке Уссури. 1969-2019 [in Russian]), 2nd edition, corrected and supplemented: album (Vladivostok: Russkii ostrov, 2019), pp.52–53.

Chapter 6

1   Authors' note: This chapter has been adapted from the article, D. S. Riabushkin, "Lake Zhalanashkol: The Last Battle of the Sino-Soviet Border War, 1969," *The Journal of Slavic Military Studies*, 33:3 (2020), pp.442-459, published online on 14 December 2020. The original article may be accessed at the website for the Taylor & Francis Group publishers at <https://www.tandfonline.com>.

2   Translator's note: the *saykan* (Chinese for 'bloody wind') is a hurricane-force wind at the Dzhungarsky Gate and Lake Alakol, blowing from Kazakhstan into China. It starts up suddenly and can last for a week.

3   A. Musalov, *Damansky and Zhalanashkol. The 1969 Sino-Soviet Armed Conflict* (Даманский и Жаланашколь. Советско-китайский вооруженный конфликт 1969 года [in Russian]) (Moscow: Izdatelskii tsentr 'Eksprint,' 2005), p.35.

4   Musalov, *Damansky and Zhalanashkol*, p.36.

5   Musalov, *Damansky and Zhalanashkol*, p.36.

6   *Krasnaya Zvezda*, 14 August 1969.

7   *Peking Review*, 12:33 (1969), p.3.

8   Petrov, *The Sino-Soviet Wars. The Truth about Damansky*, p.213.

Chapter 7

1   Authors' note: This chapter is an edited version of the article, D. S. Ryabushkin, "What They Fought with on Damanskii Island," *The Journal of Slavic Military Studies*, 19 (2006), pp.149-166. The original article may be accessed at the website for Taylor & Francis Group publishers at <https://www.tandfonline.com>.

2   Authors' note: The official Soviet names of the automatic weapon and carbine, introduced by an 18 June 1949 USSR Council of Ministers resolution and signed by Stalin, are AK and SKS, that is, they do not include the numbers 47 and 45. The names AK-47 and SKS-45 were used in Soviet technical documents only during the design and testing of these models of the weapons; these names took root in contemporary military literature, the mass media, the internet, computer games, etc.

3   Translator's note: the letter 'P' in the vehicle's name designates 'amphibious' [Russian 'plavayushchii'], and the letter 'B' designates 'turret' [Russian 'bashnya'], that is, having a conical turret with a machine gun.

Chapter 8

1   Department of State. Memorandum of Conversation, August 18, 1969, <https://nsarchive2.gwu.edu/NSAEBB/NSAEBB49/sino.sov.10.pdf> (date of access: 19 September 2020). Per Soviet tradition, second secretaries in USSR embassies were members of the special services; therefore, Davydov was probably a KGB agent.

2   Secretary of State. Memorandum for the President. Possibility of a Soviet Strike against Chinese Nuclear Facilities. September 10, 1969. <https://nsarchive2.gwu.edu/NSAEBB/NSAEBB49/sino.sov.19.pdf> (date of access: 19 September 2020).

3   M.S. Kapitsa, *At Different Parallels. Notes of a Diplomat* (На разных параллелях. Записки дипломата [in Russian]) (Moscow: AO 'Kniga i biznes,' 1996), pp.83–84.

4   See, for example, Yu.M. Galenovich, *Russia and China in the 20th Century: The Border* (Россия и Китай в XX веке: граница [in Russian]) (Moscow: Izograf, 2001), pp.159–161.

5   Galenovich, Russia and China in the 20th Century, pp.182–183.

6   <www.fmprc.gov.cn> (date of access: 15 June 2018).

Chapter 9

1   Authors' note: The PRC Academy of Social Sciences is the main research centre in China, the results of whose work are used by China's leaders. If one of the researchers from this Academy expresses scandalous ideas, then it should be understood in the following way: what the Academy researchers say, the PRC leaders think.

2   Ye. Verlin, 'For Generations to Come' (На поколения вперед [in Russian]), *Ekspert*, No. 27:238 (2000), p.36.

3   Verlin, 'For Generations to Come,' p.36.

4   Correspondence between author Dmitry Ryabushkin and V.M. Tirskikh.

5   <https://www.scmp.com/news/china/diplomacy/article/30911611/why-russias-vladivostok-celebration-prompted-nationalist> (date of access: 10 July 2020).

Appendix I

1   Translator's note: the *li*, also known as the Chinese mile, is a traditional Chinese unit of distance. Its precise length has varied over time, but usually about 1/3 of a mile. It has now been standardised to equal 500 metres.

2   Translator's note: Oirats – a western Mongol group; Uyghurs – an indigenous Turkish people of Eastern Turkestan.

3   Translator's note: bogdykhan [богдыхан] – a general term for the Chinese emperors (from the Mongolian 'boojdokhan' meaning 'sacred sovereign').

4   Translator's note: the Boxer Rebellion (Yihetuan Movement) was initiated by the Militia United in Righteousness (*Yihetuan*), known in English as the 'Boxers.' They were motivated by proto-nationalist sentiments and opposition to imperialist expansion and associated Christian missionary activity.

5   *Pravda*, 14 June 1969.

Appendix II

1   *Pravda*, 4 March 1969.

Appendix III

1 *Geroi ostrova Damanskii* [Heroes of Damansky Island] (Moscow: Molodaya gvardiya, 1969), pp.7-10.

Appendix IV

1 Authors' note: The authors were unable to find the original Russian-language version of this document. The source for this document – S. F. Ostermann, 'East German Documents on the Sino-Soviet Border Conflict, 1969,' *The Cold War in Asia*, *Cold War International History Project Bulletin*, 1995/96, Issues 6-7, pp.186-193 – provides only an English translation of this document, which is being reproduced here verbatim, including possible grammatical and punctuation errors, and differences in spellings of foreign proper nouns, word choices, style, etc., which the authors have used throughout this book.

ABOUT THE AUTHORS

Dmitry Ryabushkin

Born in the USSR, Dr. of Physics and Mathematics, Associate Professor at the Crimean Federal University named after V.I. Vernadsky. He has published five monographs and more than 50 articles in the field of physics, teaching methods, and problems of university education in Russia. He has been studying the subject of the Sino-Soviet border war since 2000. He has published four monographs on this theme: *The Myth of Damansky* [*Мифы Даманского*] in 2004; *Damansky Island. The Border Conflict. March 1969* [*Остров Даманский. Пограничный конфликт. Март 1969 года*] in 2015; *It Was on Damansky* [*Это было на Даманском*] in 2019; and *The Sino-Soviet Border Conflict of 1969* [*Советско-китайский пограничный конфликт 1969 года*] in 2020 (the original Russian-language version of this translation), as well as more than 10 articles on this subject in scholarly journals in Russia, the US, and Japan. He is recognized in Russia as one of the most objective and informative experts in the field of the history of the 1969 Sino-Soviet border conflict. This is his second publication for Helion.

Harold Orenstein

Born in the US. Received his MA and PhD in Slavic Languages from The Ohio State University. Retired since 2009 from US government service, during his 31-year career he was a translator-analyst for the Foreign Research Division of the Library of Congress; taught Russian at the US Army Russian Institute; worked as a translator, editor, and analyst for the Foreign Military Studies Office (formerly the Soviet Army Studies Office) at Fort Leavenworth, Kansas; served as a military-political analyst for Central and East European affairs at SHAPE (NATO's military branch); and served as a military analyst specialising in US joint and multinational doctrine for the Combined Arms Doctrine Directorate at Fort Leavenworth, Kansas.

He has served as the documents editor of *The Journal of Slavic Military Studies* since its founding in 1988, translating numerous Russian-language articles. His publications include the translation of seven USSR General Staff studies dealing with Soviet Army operations on the Eastern Front during the Second World War; *The Evolution of Soviet Operational Art*; *Captured Soviet Generals: The Fate of Soviet Generals Captured by the Germans*; and, most recently (2017), *The Price of Victory: The Red Army's Casualties in the Great Patriotic War*.